# FOLK
# TALES

# NORTH YORKSHIRE

# FOLK TALES

INGRID BARTON

The History Press

First published 2014

The History Press
The Mill, Brimscombe Port
Stroud, Gloucestershire, GL5 2QG
www.thehistorypress.co.uk

British Library Cataloguing in Publication Data.
A catalogue record for this book is available from the British Library.

ISBN 978 0 7524 8997 1

Typesetting and origination by The History Press
Printed in Great Britain

# CONTENTS

| | | |
|---|---|---|
| | *Story Locations* | 6 |
| | *Introduction* | 7 |
| 1 | People | 9 |
| 2 | Giants | 41 |
| 3 | Dragons | 61 |
| 4 | Creatures of the Night | 68 |
| 5 | Hobs and Such | 83 |
| 6 | Mysteries | 94 |
| 7 | Witches | 112 |
| 8 | York Stories | 132 |
| | *Notes* | 181 |

# STORY LOCATIONS

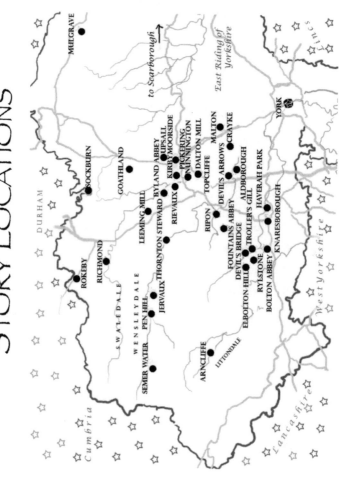

MULGRAVE

to Scarborough

East Riding of Yorkshire

YORK

SOCKBURN

GOATHLAND

UPSALL
BYLAND ABBEY
KIRBY MOORSIDE
PICKERING
NUNNINGTON
DALTON MILL
MALTON
CRAYKE
RIEVAULX
TOPCLIFFE
DEVIL'S ARROWS
ALDBOROUGH
LEEMING MILL
THORNTON STEWARD
RIPON
FOUNTAINS ABBEY
HAVERAH PARK
JERVAULX
TROLLER'S GILL
KNARESBOROUGH
DEVIL'S BRIDGE
ROKEBY
RICHMOND
ELBOLTON HILL
RYLSTONE
BOLTON ABBEY
PEN HILL
SWALEDALE
WENSLEYDALE
SEMER WATER
ARNCLIFFE
LITTONDALE

DURHAM

Cumbria

West Yorkshire

Lancashire

Lincs

# INTRODUCTION

What are folk tales? Tales told by working people and recorded by those with enough leisure, education and income to go around collecting them. The concept of 'folktale' is relatively recent. Before that, there were just stories that lived or died on the tongues of local people. It was only when they began to disappear that they suddenly became precious enough to be given a name.

In Yorkshire, as in the rest of England, there is no longer a direct line of oral storytelling tradition as there still is in Iran, Morocco or the traveller communities of Scotland. We still pass on jokes or urban myths – the buds of new folk tales – but to tell stories and develop them requires time, and time is singularly lacking in our age. The poorest agricultural worker of the past spent more time chatting to his friends and family than most of us do now (if you exclude the barrier method of the Internet).

We can no longer rely on the oral tradition, but fortunately, in Yorkshire at least, we can get some idea of the richness of that lost heritage from the work of a few men (and a couple of women) who were sufficiently interested in the common people around them to record their tales with some sympathy. They were no Brothers Grimm: collecting stories was an interest rather than a passion, however, they realised just in time that reforming clerics and the growth of schools and literacy would eventually lead to the disappearance of folk tales just as they were leading to the suppression of folk customs.

It is inevitable then that most of the stories in this book have been collected by people, mostly vicars, who were not themselves storytellers; and some bear the heavy hand of Victorian 'improvement'. I have treated them in the way any modern oral storyteller does by taking the often sketchy outline of the stories and making them my own by adding colour and details. Some people may object to my occasional use of Yorkshire dialect phrases, but Yorkshire dialect was the pithy, muscular form of speech in which the stories would originally have been told; to leave it out altogether would be to insult those old tellers. (On the other hand, if you are an expert in Yorkshire dialect I apologise for any mistakes.)

Some people do not consider historical stories, or ones about historical people, to be folk tales; I have only included ones that have a genuine folk element (i.e. they are what folk wanted to believe was true; so Archbishop Lancelot Blackburne becomes a pirate and the squalid Dick Turpin a hero).

North Yorkshire is a very large area and it has many stories, some of which are very similar (*See* Dragons). I have tried to give a broad range of the most lively ones, but there are plenty more. Folk tales are still growing out there, though slowly nowadays, rather like yew trees.

Sources for further reading can be found at the back of the book, along with notes for most of the stories.

*Ingrid Barton, 2014*

# 1

# PEOPLE

## SOMETHING TO HIS ADVANTAGE

*Hambledon Hills*

There was once a man living at Upsall in the Hambledon Hills who had a dream. In it he heard a voice saying, 'If you stand on London Bridge you will hear something to your advantage.'

The man was as poor as a church mouse so he had nothing to lose. He was also a Yorkshireman and knew better than to blab to anyone, so one day, without telling his friends or neighbours, he locked the door of his little cottage and with half a loaf of bread in his pocket, set off for London.

It was a long way so he hitched rides on passing carts, and sometimes stopped off for a day or two carrying out odd jobs to pay for his next few nights' board and lodging, but slowly he got nearer to the capital. At last he fell in with some drovers who were driving cattle to the London markets and they took him right into the city. He did not tell them about his dream and they thought him just another amiable idiot going to gawp at the sights.

For a while he did indeed enjoy walking by the mighty River Thames, impressed by the size and wealth of the buildings and the splendour of the clothes and carriages of the gentry. Then he thought, 'If I was to hear something to my advantage I could be living as high as these folk! Now where is that bridge?' Guessing that if he kept along the river he would eventually get to it, he hurried on.

His first sight of the famous London Bridge was inspiring, for this was in the days when there was only one bridge across the river and it was always crowded. There were people and horses and wagons and cattle, and even a flock of geese with tarred feet trying to cross the bridge. Those coming from the south were supposed to keep to the left, and those going out of the city to the right, but not everyone obeyed the rules and every so often a struggle would break out. There were shops and houses too, old ones, built right onto the bridge itself, leaning out over the river on both sides, so that our man was actually on it before he had realised.

'I mun be a reet gormless gavrison to have come here in first place,' said our man. 'But now I'm here I mun mak the best on it.' He pushed and shoved his way along, among all the other pushers and shovers until he had crossed the whole bridge. 'Now what?' he wondered, for though he had kept an ear out hoping to hear 'something to his advantage', he had learned nothing except some interesting new southern swearwords.

He turned back and once more crossed the bridge, but once again nothing out of the usual happened. He was losing hope now and cursed himself for an idiot as he thought of the long road home. 'Still, third time pays for all!' he thought and set off again. This time he stopped in the middle, where there was a narrow gap between one house and another. He leaned on the parapet looking out over the river.

'A fine prospect!' said a voice at his elbow. A respectable, though not richly dressed, young man stood there. 'Might I join you?'

'I suppose,' said our man suspiciously. He had heard many tales of the tricksy nature of Londoners and how they cheated poor Yorkshiremen out of their money. 'I've got no brass, tha knows,' he added bluntly.

The young man laughed, 'I assure you I have no designs on your pocket. We're not all thieves here! I can tell that you're a Yorkshireman, by your talk. I spent many years in York as a boy. It's a pleasure to hear the old accent again.'

'Oh aye.'

'Yes indeed. Fine horses, fine ale and fine lasses there. I remember it well.'

Our man was a little mollified to hear his county praised, so he moved over to let the young man lean beside him. They looked out over the river in silence for a bit, enjoying the sight of so many boats, little and big, crowding the waterway.

Finally, the young man said, 'They're talking of knocking all these old shops down and building a new bridge. It'd be a shame, don't you think?'

'Mebbe.'

'So what has brought you down to this den of iniquity from God's own county?'

Our man hesitated. 'I – well, I dreamed I should.'

'And you followed your dream. Oh my dear fellow, do you realise how fortunate you are! How I envy you!' the young man sighed, thinking of the dreary counting house where he worked and from which he dreamed of escaping. 'How I wish I might follow your example!'

'You have dreams, then?'

'Don't all men dream that life might be better?'

'An' do their dreams come true?'

'True? Alas, no. What joy to have one's dreams come true!'

'I reckon all that about dreams coming true is just shite,' said our man gloomily.

'Oh, don't say that!' spluttered his companion. 'The world would be such a terrible place if we didn't have dreams, don't you think?'

'Have you ever dreamed and it come true, then?' our man pressed on.

The young man hesitated. 'Oh, you mean dreams in your sleep? No – though, now you mention it, curiously enough I had one the other night that I hope might do so.'

'Did you now!'

'Yes, I dreamed I found a treasure!'

Our man turned and fixed him with a piercing eye.

'Oh aye?'

'I dreamed that I was in an old castle courtyard, and there was a big elder tree there.'

'That's nowt special.'

'Wait! When I dug beneath it I unearthed a huge pot of gold!'

'Now that's more like!' breathed our man. 'Pity you don't know where it was!'

'Ah, but I do – well, I remember the name, but unfortunately I've not the slightest idea where it is.' The young man sighed sadly.

'What was the name? Happen I might know it.'

'Up – something. Oh, I know; Upsall. You ever heard of it?'

'No.'

Back in Upsall his friends teased him about his prolonged absence.

'He'll have a fancy woman down there!' said one.

'No, more like he's being chased by some lass he's fathered a bairn on!' said another.

'No, no. He's been away in Pudding Pie Hill – wi' the fairies!' said a third.

Our man sat quietly and smiled. He could take jokes; he knew that they would soon be laughing on the other side of their faces.

That night he left his cottage just as if he was going for a walk – if you ignored the spade over his shoulder. The old castle of the Scropes had been abandoned since the Civil War and its gates had rotted away long ago. He peered into the courtyard with its roofless stables and piles of rubbish. Ivy was claiming the place, shooting up the keep walls and concealing in many humps and bumps the fallen stonework. It was very dark and our man had heard tales of ghosts. He clutched his spade and thought of the golden treasure.

As he looked around he thought he could see a lightness in one corner. He peered closer: white blossom. A large elder tree stood there. He strode bravely across and thrust his spade between the cobblestones beneath the tree. They put up a good resistance for a while but he was persistent and soon he was able to pull several out. Beneath them he thought he could see a dark hole.

Our man thought of giant worms and poisonous toads, but he gritted his teeth and reached into it. Almost at once he touched something cold and smooth – a box, or perhaps a pot or something. He glanced around quickly but no one was around. Swiftly he pulled it up – it was heavier than he expected and he had to use both hands – and then shoved the stones back into place. Standing up with difficulty, he hid the pot as best he could under his coat and staggered home.

In the dim light of his rush-lit cottage, our man excitedly brushed the soil off the pot. He could to see that it was ancient. On its lid there was writing. Our man was not too good at reading, but even he could see that the letters were not like the ones he had learned at dame school. He briefly wondered if it was a curse. 'In for a penny, in for a pound,' he muttered to himself with a shrug and wrenched the lid off.

There was a moment's pause, then he leapt to his feet and did a silent dance, for the rush-light now sparkled on gold; coin after coin of solid gold!

The news of our man's sudden wealth was a nine-days' wonder in the village. Some folk were pleased at his good fortune, especially as he did not move out but spent his money locally. 'He's careful, but he's not mean,' they said. Some, inevitably, were jealous, but that is the way of the world since time began, and you can be sure that the jealous ones were just as keen to be bought a pint of ale by our man as the others were. People speculated about where he had come by his fortune (was he secretly a highwayman? An alchemist?), but he said nothing, only smiled, and, as no one local had been robbed recently, in time the gossip died down.

He showed the empty pot to the vicar, hoping that he would be able to read the strange writing, but though the learned man hummed and hawed it was clear that his learning wasn't great enough. 'Some pagan druidic language, I expect,' he said.

There had seemed to be plenty of gold when our man first opened the pot, but it cost a great deal to set up the house of a wealthy man, and the same again to set up a carriage. Our man was careful, but even so the time came when the money began to run out.

Needless to say he kept the fact to himself, but soon he was living on tick and began to worry. He was going to have to borrow money and he only knew one way to do that, much though he hated the idea.

One day he surprised his coachman by giving him the day off and driving himself out alone in a little pony trap. He headed into Thirsk. Down a narrow street, he drove and knocked on an unremarkable door. A maid answered it.

'Is the Jew in?' demanded our man.

'Mr Isaac is within,' she replied coldly. 'Do you have an appointment?'

'Damn it!' spluttered our man. 'I need brass!' She led him to a comfortably furnished room where the moneylender was sitting at his desk.

'This person has come to see you,' announced the maid disdainfully. Mr Isaac saw his new client was upset, but he did not lend money just for the asking. Politely but firmly he delved delicately into his visitor's history. It was a sign of our man's desperation that, for the first time, he found himself telling the whole story.

Mr Isaac was fascinated. 'God has been good to you,' he said. 'Do you still have the ancient pot with the strange writing on it?'

'Aye, but vicar could mak nowt on it.'

'I tell you what,' said Mr Isaacs, 'I will lend you enough money to pay your immediate debts – I regret that your collateral isn't good enough for more – but the one condition is that you will show me that pot. I am a collector of antiquities in a small way. It would give me a great deal of pleasure to see it. Perhaps you might be persuaded to part with it for a suitable sum?'

And with that our man had to be satisfied.

A few days later, he returned with the pot. The old man took it to the window and inspected the writing with a large magnifying glass. He gave a short laugh. 'Very interesting!' he said.

'Oh, aye!' said our man. 'But when shall I have the money?'

Mr Isaacs put down the glass. He went back to the fire and sat down. He put the pot on his desk. 'You can't have it,' he said.

Our man's face went as red as a turkey cock. 'What? But you said! It were a bargain, spit and shake hands, you said!'

'You can't have it,' said Mr Isaacs, 'because you don't need it.'

Our man was not stupid, but at that moment, he really did look like a gormless gavrison. Mr Isaacs smiled. 'The writing is Hebraic script. Would you like to know what it says?' Our man nodded.

'It's a verse:

Look lower!
Where this stood,
Is another twice as good,

You are indeed favoured by God!'
'Keep the pot!' gasped our man, when he could speak. 'And say nowt to anyone!'

Mr Isaacs inclined his head. 'I can assure you that all our clients' affairs are treated with the upmost secrecy,' he began to say, but our man was already out of the door.

The second pot turned out to be, indeed, twice the size of the first. Our man had to take the pony trap with him when he went to get it. It had enough gold in it to last him – but who knows how much gold will be needed in a whole lifetime? Especially when you marry a willing lass and start fathering children a little late in life. Our man did not have to worry, though, for on the second pot was more strange writing – exactly the same as on the first. He knew what it meant now. He said nothing. A true Yorkshireman always likes to have a little something put away for a rainy day.

## The White Doe

### Wharfdale

It is Sunday. Folk are coming out of Bolton church when they see a white shape under the trees of the churchyard. At first they hang back, fearful of ghosts. Then, stepping lightly among the hoary gravestones, a snow-white doe comes towards them. It stops at a safe distance and regards them with its great brown eyes, poised to run.

The churchgoers give it a wide berth, but the next Sunday it is there again – and the next. Sunday after Sunday, it returns, now standing further back, by the graves of the Norton family. Folk agree that it is no natural deer, with its sad eyes, but appearing as it does on the Lord's Day, neither can it be evil. No one attempts to drive it away.

Soon the gossip had a sighting at Rylstone church too. There is speculation as to whose ghost it might be, some favouring one deceased candidate and some another, but most agree that it is the fetch of Emily Norton, come to mourn at her brothers' grave. 'A sad tale,' they agree.

Richard Norton had nine tall sons, archers and swordsmen all. They lived at Rylstone Hall and had a hunting lodge, Norton Tower, near Rylstone Fell where they stayed at times to hunt the red deer. He also had one daughter, Emily, who was quiet and pale and devout.

Among so many boisterous men Emily was often forgotten or neglected, left behind when they went hunting (for she would not join them) and silent as a mouse at the table where they talked loudly of their exploits. She loved them fiercely though: their easy grace on horseback, their rough playful ways and their good spirits. Best of all she loved to see them when they all knelt together at prayers in the evening, silent and respectful for once; a row of brothers united by their religion, a strong wall protecting the family.

She had a particular fondness for her eldest brother Francis and he returned it in the careless way of young men. He often brought her little presents, but one day he surpassed himself by bringing out from under his cloak a little fawn: a white one. It was tiny, bleating feebly.

'A white deer is good luck!' he told her. 'I've never seen another. I thought you would make a good mother for it.'

Emily kissed him happily, though she soon learned the hard way what it is to care for another creature's baby. The little fawn could go for a long time without food, but the moment that it smelt milk it would begin to struggle to its feet, and its bleating grew loud and shrill. The old family shepherd showed her the trick of putting her hand in the milk and getting the fawn to suck her fingers to persuade it to drink by itself.

The fawn survived and began to grow into a fine doe. It followed Emily wherever she went; they became inseparable.

But times were changing. Richard and his children did not realise how much. They were shocked to hear that King Henry had decided to put away his true wife, Catherine, and marry his whore, Anne Bullen. How was it possible for a marriage – especially one of such a long duration – to be dissolved on a whim?

Worse was to follow, for the king, no doubt influenced by bad council, foreigners and above all his base-born chancellor, Cromwell, seemed determined to break with the Holy Father in Rome and bring damnation upon the whole country.

The male portion of the family debated and argued at table and away from it. They were united in their determination not to change their faith in any way. 'How can a king change what God has ordained?' they asked. In this, they shared the opinion of most of their neighbours in the North. What they could not agree on was what to do about it. The younger hotheads were all for local landowners raising troops and riding to London to demand that the king change his evil advisors. Older and wiser heads pointed out that this king was not a man who brooked criticism from anyone. 'Your heads would decorate London Bridge before your feet were out of the stirrups!' said their father.

Francis said, 'The king listens to arguments. We should write to him setting out our points carefully.' But the other sons laughed at him, saying that they were not lawyers but the sons of a gentleman. In the end, the wiser councils prevailed and nothing was done – for the moment.

Meanwhile Emily's doe was fully grown. She saw that the time had come for her pet to return to the herd and that it would be cruel to keep her a prisoner. She knew that her brothers would never kill her doe and so one day she took her into the deer park, where the herd was feeding. The doe trembled with excitement when she saw others of her kind and tentatively approached the herd. A fine stag caught her scent and came trotting out to meet and claim her. Emily returned home a little sad, but knowing that she had done the best she could for her friend. In the years following Emily often saw the doe running with the herd; flashing in the sunlight as the deer streamed along a hill or shimmering white among the trees of the wood, but they did not approach each other again.

One day a neighbour came galloping to the gates of Rylstone Hall. He brought news that, at first, no one could believe: the king had ordered commissioners to investigate all monasteries and decide whether they were being properly administered. They had the power to close any that were found wanting.

'It's just an excuse invented by court lawyers for stealing the Church's property!' declared Richard.

'Like enough it's the king who will eat the goods,' said Christopher, another of the sons. 'He grows as fat as Pig Ellen – and as greedy!'

His father struck him for insulting the king, but his view was silently held by many. The news soon spread to the commoners and they were consumed with fear. If the monasteries closed, who would help to feed the poor in times of famine? Who would provide them with care when they were ill? Who would keep the powers of darkness at bay?

The great landowners of the North and their people were never friends of change. They wished to live the life that their forefathers had lived, safe in the certainties that had sustained them for centuries: their religion, administered by priests in the magic language, Latin; the social hierarchy where everyone knew their place, their responsibilities, their obligations. New ideas, new men, new practices they rejected as dangerous to order, and order, in a troubled region like the North, was thought more important than anything.

Emily heard talk of a pilgrimage as she sat at the family table. It would not be to a holy place but it would be a holy thing itself, formed of abbots, priests, lords and ordinary people. They would go to London humbly and prayerfully to beg the king to spare the monasteries and, by ridding himself of certain evil councillors, to make his people happy.

It seemed to Emily to be a good idea. Surely the king could not refuse a request from so many good people? Francis alone held out against the family joining the 'Pilgrimage of Grace', because he did not trust the king – or any king for that matter.

'Henry will see this as rebellion and use it as a reason to break the power of our northern lords. No king can bear rivals and we northerners have trodden on his toes once too often.'

His father and his brothers ignored his view, saying that they were ready to die for their religion if necessary. In the end it was decided that Francis could remain behind to care for the estate, while father and sons went south with the Pilgrimage.

Day after day passed by without any news reaching Rylstone Hall. One day, Emily and Francis rode out together to view the deer. It was the season of the rut; rival stags were belling out their challenges to each other and then rushing together again and again with a great clash of antlers. Emily could not see her white doe. She shivered in the brisk wind.

'God protect our father and brothers!' she murmured.

'Amen' her brother replied, but he looked troubled.

News began at last to dribble in. It seemed that the Pilgrimage had not reached London. It had met the king's forces and there had been a stand-off, neither wishing to fight the other. Perhaps if one of those great Northern lords had been prepared to take charge the king might have been forced to grant some of their requests, but none did, and so at the first mention of a pardon for all who departed quietly, men began to drift away. Richard and his sons returned angry and humiliated.

The monasteries closed. Bolton Abbey was despoiled and its treasures carried away by men who suddenly became rich. Only the monastery church remained in use, a simple parish church now. Time passed. The old king died and went to be judged by God. His young son, a fierce Protestant but mercifully a weakling, died soon after. At last, Mary, a true Catholic queen, came to restore the land. Around Rylstone people breathed more freely, now the old ways would return, they said. Some of the Norton family agreed with them. Others, like Francis, were not so sure. As time went on, the new queen did not thrive. She had no children; she was ill. Men said she was wasting away. Now all the Nortons were alarmed. The next in line to the throne was another Protestant, the bastard Elizabeth. Surely the followers of the true religion must stop her taking the throne!

Upon Mary's passing, Elizabeth was crowned. She showed no intention of undoing the evil her father had done. She pretended to be gracious and forgiving, but it was only a matter of time, thought the Nortons, before she remembered the Northern lords and wished to bring them to heel.

There was no talk of persuasion. Force of arms, they decided, was the only way to remove this upstart queen and replace her with her Catholic cousin, Mary, Queen of Scots. Now free speech at dinner in front of servants or women ceased. Emily heard whispering, doors closed on her and there was an atmosphere of conspiracy. She knew they were planning rebellion and fear grew in her heart. Her brothers asked her to make a banner for them, embroidered with the five wounds of Christ. They began to practise more with sword and buckler. They almost abandoned hunting in favour of polishing off their fighting skills.

Emily implored Francis to tell her what was happening, but he shook his head and said that the time was not yet ripe. She took to visiting her mother's grave in Rylstone church to pray for her family.

Then there was a day of bags being packed, of whinnying horses being groomed and harnessed. Men she did not know gathered in the courtyard. Her father called her into the parlour and kissed her. He told her that he and eight of her brothers were going to join an armed rebellion led by the Earls of Westmoreland and Northumberland.

'You must be a brave lass and keep the hall while we are gone.'

'Is Francis going with you?'

'He is, but only as my squire. He says he will not fight against the queen, foolish lad. We shall see!' replied her father.

They rode away in great style, her father and her nine brothers, proud beneath the banner she had worked for them. What could she do but pray for their safe return?

Her prayers were destined not to be answered.

Once again, a neighbour on a sweating horse galloped to the gates of Rylstone Hall with news, but this time his eyes were red with weeping.

'Mistress Emily, you must be brave,' he began, and Emily knew that all was lost. White as her own doe, she led him into the hall and sat with him at the empty table while he told her of the failure of the rebellion; of the capture of her father and brothers.

'The Queen's Grace now says that all those who went on the Pilgrimage of Grace have forfeited by this uprising the pardon given to them by her father. She will have blood, Mistress Emily. Her anger is terrible, they say.'

'Are my father and brothers then, dead? I thought them only captured.' He hesitated.

'They live yet, mistress, but in prison and condemned to be hanged for treason.'

Emily stared at the wall before her, still as an alabaster monument.

'And what of my brother Francis? Was he also taken? He swore he would not fight!'

The neighbour looked down at his hands and said nothing.

'Speak!'

'Your brother Francis did not fight, they say, but when your brothers and father were taken he picked up their standard, the one that bore the five wounds of Christ, and escaped with it. But as he rode past Bolton Priory, Sir George Bowes and his henchmen met with him by accident and, thinking to gain favour with the queen, slew him …'

She fell forward onto the table as though he had struck her with a hammer. The neighbour shouted for the servants who chafed her hands and temples and laid her in bed. 'Your message has surely killed her!' they said, but she was not dead. Next day she rose from her bed to begin her duties as the head of the shattered household.

Her first duty was to find Francis' body and bring it home for burial, but even that was denied to her, for his killers, struck with guilt perhaps, had had him buried in the churchyard at Bolton Priory. She rode over there as soon as she felt strong enough and spent many hours praying by the newly piled earth that marked his grave.

A cold winter's day brought a group of six men on tired horses into her courtyard. They were heavily cloaked and led three pack mules bearing three black sinister loads. Though they were muffled up to the eyes, Emily had no sooner caught sight of them than she ran weeping to meet them, for she recognised some of the brothers that she thought lost forever.

They told her that though their father and her brothers Christopher and Thomas had been executed, the king had shown mercy to six of them. 'We have brought the others back with us to lie in their own land,' they told her. They decided to bury their dead at Bolton Priory next to their brother.

Now the wrath of the queen broke over the North like a tidal wave. Anyone who had been involved in the Pilgrimage of Grace was to be punished. Hangmen had never been so busy; in every town and village known to have taken part people were hanged; lords, knights and gentlemen died as well as commoners.

The Norton family had only a little time together before the final blow struck them. Their father, having been hanged as a traitor, had forfeited his estates to the Crown. Soon the sequestrator arrived with his men to take possession and the remaining Nortons had to leave their family home. They were destitute, forced to rely on their neighbours for shelter and the very food they ate.

The remaining Norton brothers no longer dared remain in England. Being young and active they went abroad to seek their fortune in foreign wars, but their sister refused to go with them. She became a wanderer, freely offered shelter and sustenance by those who still clung stubbornly to the old faith. She walked the moors in all weathers from cottage to cottage, unwilling to be a burden for too long. Sometimes she walked to Bolton church, the only part of its monastery to remain in use. She could often be seen there as months turned into years, praying in the nave or by the graves of her father and brothers.

One day she could bear the separation from her old home no longer. She walked the long miles to Rylstone to sit once more in the deer park near Norton Tower where she and her brothers had once played.

As she rested under an oak tree and looked around at the familiar landscape, she saw, beyond the yellow summer gorse, a herd of deer. There was a white one among them, who seemed to be watching her. Slowly, cautiously, it left the herd and came towards her. Trembling with something like hope, Emily held out her hand. Gracefully the white doe stepped up to her and bent its head to lick her salty palm. Then, with a sigh, it settled itself down beside her just as it had when it was a fawn. Emily, comforted at last, wept for her lost family as she had never been able to before.

From that day on the two became once more inseparable. Their two souls drew closer together until they seemed like one. Lonely shepherds grew familiar with the sight of them walking slowly, gracefully together along the top of a hill or drinking at a moorland pool as they travelled between the churches of Bolton and Rylstone. On moonlit nights, they might be seen sleeping curled in the bracken or sheltering from rain below the rocks of Rylstone crag.

How long do deer live? Longer than Emily, it seems. Her hard life and grief soon wore down what was left of her youth and health. She died long before her time and was buried by her former neighbours next to her mother in Rylstone church. Not long afterwards, the white doe was seen for the first time on its own at Bolton. Some folk believed

that Emily's soul, unable to bear leaving the graves of her family even for the joys of heaven, returned again and again in the ghostly form of the white doe. But it may be that her lonely, unquiet soul still clung to that of the living friend of her youth until the white doe too lay down to sleep for the last time by Norton Tower.

## POTTER THOMPSON

*Swaledale*

On the banks of the Swale rises a huge rock on which the old market town of Richmond stands. A poor man by the name of

Potter Thompson once lived there. He made the simple pancheons and jugs used by dairymaids up and down the dale, and sold them in the market or carried them up Swaledale loaded on his old donkey. It was a hard life, for his pots sold very cheaply and he had a nagging wife to support; she was always telling him how lazy and stupid he was. He was a cheerful man nevertheless, especially when he was away from home, and Richmond folk were fond of him, though, as they said, he would never set the Swale on fire.

When his wife's tongue drove him out of the house, he would wander about town hoping that someone would buy him a beer, or he would stroll down to the river and enjoy the sight and sound of the swirling water.

One day, when his wife was more than usually angry at the pittance he had brought home from the market, he stomped down to the river to cool off, for he had answered her back, which was always fatal. It was a cold and windy day. The river was the colour of tea, made so by the ironstone upstream – no, not tea, he thought, more like beer with the curling cream foam on it. 'A river of beer!' he thought. 'Now that would be a thing to see!' He fell into a happy dream imagining it.

The path he was on went right along the foot of the castle rock. He had been on it many times, but suddenly he woke from his beery daydream staring at a narrow black hole in the rocks that he had never seen before.

'What's this?' he wondered to himself, peering into its depths. The stories his grandmother used to tell him came into his mind: smugglers' tunnels, highwaymen's caches, treasure caves. A feeling of recklessness that he thought had been nagged out long ago seized him. 'I could just squeeze in there,' he thought. 'Now is my chance to be a hero!' He saw an image of himself emerging from the hole bearing a chest of gold. 'I will go in!'

Gingerly he pushed himself into the opening. It was dark. So very dark.

'Fool!' he thought. 'I haven't got any matches – or a candle, for that matter! Fine treasure seeker I am!' He was standing there in the dark, wondering whether he should go and get a lantern or just go on anyway, when he noticed that the darkness did not seem as black as he had first thought. Some sort of light was coming from the end of what he now saw was a long tunnel. Nothing terrible had happened to him so far, so he plucked up his courage and, bending low to avoid projecting rocks, he crept along the tunnel. He felt more alive than he had for years!

The illumination grew stronger as he went and he could now see it was not the cold light of day, but a warmer, pearly light. The air was warmer too, pleasant after the cold wind outside. The way led downwards. Soon he noticed that the roof of the tunnel was growing further away and the tunnel itself was opening out into a cave. He hesitated. 'Might be a dragon or anything in there,' he thought, listening hard and glancing nervously back over his shoulder. 'Still, it's not too far to run if I need to.'

Bravely he stepped forwards into a huge chamber, right underneath the castle, as far as he could guess. At first he could see nothing but a stony floor littered with fallen rocks. He heard a strange, repetitive sound that he could not quite place. Then his eyes seemed to refocus and he could see that in the middle of the cavern was a stone table. Something on the table glinted and the pearly light appeared to be coming from that object.

'There really is treasure!' he breathed. Walking carefully, trying to avoid the huge rocks, he moved towards the light. On the table was a great horn of ivory, bound with silver and inlaid with gold. Next to it was a magnificent sword in a richly decorated scabbard. Jewels flashed in the hilt: blood-red rubies, amethysts the colour of violets, topazes as yellow as the sun.

Potter Thompson's hand went out to grasp it, but it seemed so magical that he did not quite dare. Surely, these treasures were not for a poor man like himself? And, more importantly, surely they were guarded by someone or something? He looked around fearful of some unseen threat and as his eyes passed over the rock-strewn floor, he realised that the stones were not rocks at all, but men, huge sleeping men in armour. The strange sound was their soft rhythmic breathing.

In a sudden flash Potter knew who they were. His grandmother had often told him how, after the Battle of Camlann, King Arthur

and his men had been put into a magic sleep inside a cave to await the day when they would arise to help Britain in the hour of her greatest need. He could remember clearly the firelight flickering on his grandmother's face and hear her soft old voice respond when he asked the location of the cave. 'Why, some folk think it were right here in Richmond! In a big cavern under the castle!'

He was so excited that he actually laughed, but so alarmingly the sound echoed off the walls that he was afraid it would wake the sleepers. Instinctively, he knew that if there was one thing he must not do, it was to awaken them. Their breathing was soft, but it was the only soft thing about them for it was clear that they were men of war. Each man was at least seven feet tall. They were wearing coats of mail with their swords laid to their hands and their shields under their heads. Helmets, some ornamented with boars' tusks and some with horse tails, lay nearby. Their hands were the scarred fists of warriors and their faces, though relaxed in sleep, were stern. The magic in which they were wrapped was so strong that Potter Thompson could feel it prickling his skin, making him shiver.

Lying in the centre of the men was another, larger and older than the rest. He was clean-shaven, and had such an air of sorrow about him that Potter Thompson felt his own eyes filling with tears as he looked at him. On the man's head was a golden crown. There was no mistaking him.

'King Arthur his very self!' breathed Potter Thompson. 'And me, Potter Thompson! I've seen him! Me, who's never done aught before! Just think of it! So much for your opinion!' he said, thinking of his wife. 'You can keep your great flapping trap shut from now on!' He began to imagine telling her of his discovery and straight away his joy diminished. 'She'll never credit it,' he thought. 'No more will the others.' He could almost hear the jeering of his drinking mates. 'I'll have to take something back with me as proof.' But what?

The obvious choice lay on the table. 'Excalibur!' he gasped. 'I'll take 'em Excalibur!'

He turned again to the table, holding his breath as he put out his hand. As he grasped the hilt, it was as though all the years of his adulthood flowed backwards and he was a daring schoolboy again. To draw Excalibur! What an adventure!

As he began to ease the sword out of its scabbard, all of the sleepers began to stir and breathe more quickly. In terror, he thrust it back again. After a brief, horrible moment, the sleepers relaxed again and the regular breathing filled the cavern once more.

Reluctantly Potter Thompson realised that he would have to abandon Excalibur. 'I'll take that horn at any rate,' he said to himself, reaching out for it. This time it was worse. As soon as he touched it, the warriors began to stir again. Some muttered in their sleep and one or two even began to sit up and fumble for their swords.

It was too much for Potter Thompson. He dropped the horn, turned and ran. Down the long tunnel he crashed, blundering into walls and banging his head. As he ran he heard a voice singing, though whether it was behind him or in the walls themselves he could not tell. The words remained burned into his memory:

> Potter Thompson, Potter Thompson
> If thou hadst either drawn
> The sword or wound the horn
> Then thou hadst been the luckiest man
> That ever yet was born!

His wife was amazed when he came home shaking and bleeding from a hundred scrapes and scratches. For once she did not scold him but put him to bed with a hot brick at his feet. He slept like a log for a whole day.

His wife's kindness proved just a temporary lapse, but Potter Thompson himself was never quite the same man again, though his life seemed to go back to its normal dull routine. His friends did not exactly believe his story, but they could not help feeling a little proud of him and there were few weeks when he was not to be found sitting in the alehouse, a free pint in his fist, being encouraged to tell his tale to wondering strangers.

'You wait,' he used to say to his friends, 'one day I'll go back in there and bring you proof!' But he could never find the entrance again and they are all still waiting …

## The Drummer Boy

### Swaledale

On top of Richmond rock stands not just the town of Richmond but a fine medieval castle, built, it is said, by William the Conqueror. Long after it ceased to be used to guard the city it got a new lease of life as the home of the local militia. A barracks was built inside the curtain walls and the echoes of trumpets were once again thrown back by the ancient stone.

Everyone knew Potter Thompson's story by this time, though he himself was long dead. Children told each other about it and spent the summer (as my own children did 200 years later) searching for the entrance to his wonderful cave. His was not the only story they told each other, though – there was said to be a treasure hidden beneath the Gold Hole tower and the secret tunnel that leads to Easby Abbey. If only you could get into the castle itself, they thought, who knows what you might find? If only the soldiers were not there …

The soldiers heard these stories too and were just as keen as the children to search for some way into the secret places of the rock. One day a group of soldiers was sent down to the dungeons to clear space for the storage of gunpowder. The opportunity to explore was too good to miss: they had plenty of candles with them and, once they had moved some of the rubbish accumulated over centuries, they started to search in good earnest for secret passages.

'What would you do if we found the cave? Take the sword or blow the horn?' Fred asked Bill.

'I don't mind,' said Bill, 'as long we wake up some decent soldiers. Happen they'll fight the French instead of us.'

'Well, I hope those old fellers down there know how to fire a musket, then!' laughed Fred.

'I don't want to wake the old knights,' chipped in the twelve-year-old drummer boy named Georgie, who was searching with them. 'I just want to become the luckiest person that ever was born!' They went from cellar to cellar, dungeon to dungeon, lower and lower until they could go no further.

'I reckon we've had it now,' said another of the soldiers. 'There's no more doors. Let's get back. It's almost muster time.'

'What's that behind that old pillar?' said another. They held their candles closer.

'Damn me if it isn't a hole!' said Bill. 'And look, you can just see that it's living rock beyond, not squared stones!' They all knelt and jostled for a good view.

Fred whistled. 'I think it widens out. This is it, lads. We've found the way in!'

'And how do you think we're going to explore it, mate?' Fred said, gloomily. 'You'll never squeeze your fat belly in there, and neither will I!' The men all looked at each other in dismay. One or two lay down and tried to edge themselves through the narrow hole, but it was a tight fit and no one dared take the risk of ending up in the dark, unable to squeeze back out.

'Who's the smallest of us?' asked Fred. All eyes slowly turned to Georgie. He was certainly smaller than any of the adults, and rather puny for his age.

'Now's your chance, lad!' said Bill. 'Go in and bring us back some treasure!'

Georgie looked at the black hole and gulped. 'Isn't that the trumpet for muster?' he stammered. 'I'll go tomorrow.'

'Nay, lad,' the others said. 'Tomorrow'll be too late. We'll never be let down here again. It's now or never. Where's your courage?'

'Where's *your* courage!' he retorted, but at the same time he was becoming more excited, for it was true, he was the only one small enough to squeeze through the hole. What a story to tell his mates! He'd be a hero. 'Well, all right,' he said, 'but I need some snap and some candles.'

A soldier ran to fetch what he needed, sneaking a loaf of bread and a black bottle of beer from the quartermaster's stores. The others added whatever candles they had left. Soon Georgie's feet slithered out of sight and the men pushed the pack after him.

'What's it like?' they asked.

'I can stand up,' came the muffled reply. 'Wait while I light the candle.' They heard him striking his flint and steel, and a few minutes later they all heard him say, 'There's a tunnel goes right on, horrible and dark. I'm frit though. I'm coming back.' The soldiers groaned.

'Wait, lad,' said Bill. 'That's no good. Don't you want to know where it goes? Look, I'll push your drum through. You can play that, marching like, and it'll stop you being frit. Give us a few minutes to go outside and with any luck, we'll be able to hear you. That way we can follow you above ground and see where you stop.' He pushed the drum through the hole and heard it bang against the tunnel wall as Georgie slung it around his neck.

'How can I hold the candle and drum as well?'

'Stick the candle on your hat like a miner,' someone suggested. 'Come on, Georgie. We'll all be so proud of you. Just think, no one has gone inside this rock since the days of Potter Thompson, and he were never as brave and clever as you.'

'Aye, I've done that then,' said Georgie, after a moment. 'Stuck it on the peak of my cap. I can see better now. Well, I'll be off. I'll come back here if I get stuck. I'm going to beat the Advance.'

He began to drum, playing the call known as the Advance: rat-tat-tat *ta*-tat rat-tat-tat and the listening soldiers heard him move off down the tunnel. They ran up to the light of the courtyard and listened. Yes! Distantly they could still hear the drum below their feet: rat-tat-tat *ta*-tat rat-tat-tat. It headed across the yard and through the gate into the town.

'Happen he's found the tunnel that goes to Easby,' Bill guessed. But alas, they were all soldiers with duties inside the walls of the castle, not free men who might go wherever they wanted. The sentry on guard at the gate refused to let them leave, despite their pleas, and their officer, coming up, threatened them all with a flogging if they did not get to muster immediately.

In the evening when they were off duty, they tried to locate the sound of the drum again, wandering about the ancient town, pressing their ears to walls or the ground. Folk stared at them, but they did not care. Every so often, they would hear a rat-tat-tat, always in a different place, as though the boy were wandering round and round. Now it was right next to the castle, now near the town gate or beneath the Buck Inn. Fred sneaked back down to the cellars and shouted himself hoarse down the narrow hole into which the poor lad had disappeared, but there was no response.

The soldiers tried the next day and the next. The drumming, when they caught the sound of it, seemed still to continue as strongly as before. It was as though Georgie needed no rest. Day after day, they pursued the sound, quite prepared to try digging him out if only he would stop, but he never ceased to beat or to move forward. Georgie the drummer boy was never seen again by anyone in Richmond, nor by his distraught family in Swaledale.

As the years went by, local folk would hear the sound of the drum from time to time and would put their fingers in their ears as their blood ran cold; surely, the poor little lad must have died of hunger and thirst long ago? It is said that even now on still winter evenings, when the shops are shut and all the visitors and their cars have gone home, you may hear, deep beneath you feet, the sound of a lonely drum playing the Advance: rat-tat-tat *ta*-tat rat-tat-tat, as Georgie continues his solitary march …

## LAME HAVERAH

*Knaresborough*

Long before the Paralympic games, disabled people had to develop great physical skill and stamina just to survive. With only simple aids, such as crutches, they had to find work, or beg, or starve. There were few alternatives, for life was very hard. It is not surprising, therefore, that when Lame Haverah of Knaresborough met John of Gaunt by chance he grasped his opportunity with both hands.

John was Duke of Lancaster, and among his many other possessions, owned the Forest of Knaresborough. One windy autumn day when he was hunting there with his men, he came across Lame Haverah hopping along on his crutches. Almost automatically, the duke stopped to give alms to the poor man, but to his surprise Haverah seized his outstretched hand and, kneeling on the ground, begged him for a boon. The huntsmen moved to drive off this upstart, but Duke John stopped them.

'What is it you want? If it is in my power I will grant it,' he said, thinking that it would be some small thing – food, perhaps – suitable to what he imagined were the needs of a poor cripple. He was taken aback when the young man said, 'Grant me some land, my lord!'

The duke's men shook their heads and murmured at this effrontery, but the sheer nerve of the man amused the great lord.

'What is your name?'

'Haverah, if it please you, my lord.'

'Very well, Haverah,' said Lord John. 'Listen to what I vow! I, John of Gaunt, Do give and grant, To thee Haverah, As much of my ground, As thou canst hop around, In a long summer's day! Next St Bartholomew's Day I will return and we shall see how well you can hop!' Lord John said, whilst thinking to himself that 'He'll at least get enough for a little house and vegetable plot, and we'll all have a good laugh at his antics as well!'

Haverah thanked him effusively with tears in his eyes and hopped away to plan how to make the most of his good fortune.

There were no gyms or personal trainers in those days (at least not for anyone lower than the rank of knight), but in the months that followed Haverah tried as hard as he could to prepare himself for the ordeal. His wooden crutches were just a stick of wood and a rough crosspiece to fit under his shoulder. The crutches gave him blisters on his hands and in his armpits. Haverah scoured the forest for two branches that forked comfortably at the end and wadded them well with sheep's wool gathered from the hedges and made into pads by his mother. He strengthened his arms by pulling himself up on doorframes or beams. By the following June, he was as ready as he would ever be.

His whole village turned out just before dawn on St Bartholomew's Day (24 June). The news had spread to other villages and, even though it was so early, there was a sizeable crowd to witness the extraordinary event. Duke John, as he had promised, was there with some of his friends. He also brought plenty of food and servants to serve it.

The day dawned bright and hot and as soon as the sun began to peep over the hills, Haverah began his hop, swinging along on the new crutches.

Those watching were amazed at how swiftly he moved, covering the ground almost as fast as an able-bodied man could run. The villagers, always on the side of the underdog, cheered him on; Duke John's friends began to lay bets on how long he would last.

'Surely he can't keep that up,' muttered Duke John, looking worried.

By midday, Haverah was panting and the sweat was dripping into his eyes, but he did not stop to wipe it away. He was still moving fast and had already covered a surprisingly large distance.

Duke John's friends were slapping the great lord's back and laughing at him instead of Haverah now. He emptied his goblet of wine gloomily. 'He's sped his bolt,' he said. 'He can't last much longer.'

The duke was wrong. Though the pain of his shoulders and hands was almost unbearable, though his legs burned like fire and his breath came in great gasps, Haverah kept going all afternoon

and into the early evening. The sun was sinking low as, surrounded by cheering villagers – some of whom had run all the way with him – Haverah staggered towards the place where he had started. As the sun slipped beneath the horizon, he collapsed on the ground. He was too exhausted to laugh, but he smiled.

'So how much land are you really going to give him?' drawled one of Duke John's friends. 'Surely not the whole amount? It's big enough to make a knight a fine deer park!'

'I'm a knight and I made him a promise! We have our standards, damn it!' growled the duke. 'Well, let him have the land. He's earned it – but let us never speak of this matter again!' So they never did.

Thus Haverah acquired the great parcel of land now called Haverah Park, and it brought him and his mother enough money to live as wealthy people for the rest of their lives.


# ROBIN HOOD AND THE CURTAL FRIAR

*Harrogate area*

These days Robin Hood is usually connected with Sherwood Forest, but in older stories he is more often to be found in Barnsdale, West Yorkshire. However, as the number of wells, stones and caves (not to mention Robin Hood's Bay near Whitby) named after him shows, there were also occasions when he ventured into the North and East Ridings.

Imagine the greenwood: a forest of huge craggy oak trees. Imagine them covered in the pale-green leaves of spring. Imagine deer stealthily appearing and disappearing among their shadows or standing still with one foot delicately raised. See there, a large buck silently crosses a grassy track; its hide flashing a rich brown in a little pool of sunlight. Listen, there is a whirring sound, the buck leaps and falls dead with an arrow in its heart. There are hunters in the greenwood.

Far down the track, two men come loping towards its body.

'That was a mighty shot, John!' says Robin Hood. 'I don't remember ever seeing a better!' Little John smiles.

'It was a fair shot,' he agrees, 'but I know a man who could easily better it. A friar, no less – a curtal friar.' Robin is immediately interested.

'A friar who can shoot! That would be a sight to see. I thought that they just went around begging, seducing women and filling their big bellies.'

'I don't know about the wives, but he certainly has the belly. He's a brawler too and as good with the quarterstaff as he is with the bow.'

'Sounds just like the sort of man we could use,' says Robin. 'Friars ramble about all over the country. Where can he be found?'

'At the moment he's staying with the monks at Fountains Abbey. Whether he'd be interested in joining us, I don't know. Let's get this deer back to camp and then go and see!'

Friar Tuck is strolling by the River Skell digesting a venison pasty. He is a fine figure of a man; with a large paunch, certainly, but well-muscled and sturdy with mischievous eyes. He is twirling a long staff and humming a popular tune. Suddenly, from the grass in front of him, a man in Lincoln green rises up.

'Good morrow, Friar!' says the man. 'I wonder whether you could help me.'

'Certainly, my son,' says the friar jovially. 'Trouble with your love life?'

Robin smiles. 'No, something much easier to solve. I need to get to the other side of the river without wetting my feet. Will you oblige me by carrying me over?'

The friar raises his eyebrows and considers the man in front of him. 'Why, certainly,' he says. 'Jump aboard!' He kilts up his robe. Robin jumps onto his back and hangs on round his neck. Carefully leaning on his staff the friar descends waist-deep into the river and wades across, making light of his heavy burden. At the other side, he sets Robin down.

'Just before you go –' he says as Robin seems about to turn away. 'I'm now on the wrong side of the river. As you can see, the monastery is on the other side. One good turn deserves another, my son. It's only fair that you carry me back!'

Robin considers the bulky friar with alarm. 'But my shoes …'

'Worldly vanity, my son. You can always take them off.'

Robin does not want to seem a weakling, so he bends forward. 'Certainly I will carry you, good father. Hop up!'

Hopping is not what the friar is built to do, but he clambers onto Robin's back. Robin staggers, hardly able to stand, but he slithers down into the unpleasantly cold water. The friar seems determined to annoy him. He spurs him on with kicks and cries of 'Gee up Bayard!'

If it were not for Robin's own staff, he probably would not be able to get across, but he makes it and heaves himself up onto the bank. He shakes the friar off.

'Well done old nag!' laughs the friar, slapping him heavily on the back. 'You'd make a fine plough stot!' He turns to go.

'Just a moment, Father!' Robin thumps his quarterstaff menacingly.

'Yes, my son? Do you want me to pray for you?' Robin grinds his teeth.

'No, thank you. But as you see it is I who am now on the wrong side of the river. Be so good as to carry me back!' He stares at the friar in a less than friendly manner.

'Wrong side? Oh yes, so you are. Well, my son, we must remedy that immediately. Up you get!'

Once again, Robin gets on the friar's back and he wades into the river. This time it is Robin who shouts 'Gee up!' He is enjoying himself!

In the middle of the river his mount stops. 'Get on, Dobbin!'

With a wild neigh, the friar bucks him off into the river. Robin goes under and comes up angry and spitting. He is even more angry when he sees his hat gaily floating away down the river and he hears the friar's loud laughter.

'Right!' he growls, making a hasty grab for his quarterstaff before it follows his hat. He struggles up the bank, water pouring off him.

'I'm waiting for you, my son!' chortles the friar, twirling his staff so fast that it is just a blur.

They come together with a great crash; their quarterstaffs flash and whirl through the air like lightning, splinters and chips of wood fly from them. The woods of Fountains Abbey resound with the noise and disturbed birds flap away. Occasionally there is a thump and a grunt as a blow strikes home.

Little John has been right about the friar's skill. Both men are well matched: Robin is quicker on his feet, but the friar has the advantage of extra weight in his blows and soon weight begins to tell. They draw back now to regain their breath, leaning panting on their staffs. Robin knows that it is only a matter of time before the friar beats him. He is only just able to deflect strikes that would crack his skull if they landed.

'Friar!' he calls. 'Grant me a request! Let me just blow three blasts on my horn!'

The friar laughs. 'Blow till your eyes pop out! Much good may it do you!'

Robin blows three blasts and before the valley has ceased echoing, fifty men in Lincoln green come running from their hiding places in trees and bushes. They all have bows with arrows on the string.

'O ho! That's how it is, is it?' exclaims the friar. 'In that case grant me a request! Let me whistle three times!'

'Whistle till your cheeks burst!'

The friar puts his fingers to his lips and whistles. From the abbey grounds on the third whistle come fifty great dogs, baying as they run. They charge down upon the outlaws who immediately begin to shoot at them.

Now here is a strange sight! The dogs are so clever that they dodge the arrows and bring them back to the friar in their mouths. The outlaws are amazed. Soon they will have no more arrows.

'Stop! Enough!' shouts Robin, laughing in spite of himself. 'My men need their arrows! What a man you are, Friar! My respect to you!'

The friar mops his sweating face with his robe. 'It was a good fight,' he says. 'My guess is that you are Robin Hood! I was hoping to

stumble across you.' Robin bows. 'I am indeed and I would like to offer you a place in my band if you would like it. I've never seen such a fighter – and I'm sure the dogs would come in handy.'

The friar considers. 'Come to the greenwood, eh? Well, we friars are supposed to preach to the poor. I might be able to bring some smattering of holy learning to you poor benighted souls. But tell me first, do you have venison pasties in the forest?'

'Of course! What else are the king's deer for?'

The friar smiles broadly. 'Then Friar Tuck is your man. Lead on!'

# 2

# GIANTS

## ON GIANTS

In the days before Darwin, people imagined their ancestors to have been much bigger than themselves; after all they were closer to the hand of God than we dwellers in degenerate times. Surely they must have been giants of men and women, not just larger but stronger, braver and more skilled than their feeble descendants! When King Arthur's bones were conveniently discovered by the monks of Glastonbury in the twelfth century, no one was surprised that they were of giant size, indeed, that was considered proof that they really were Arthur's bones.

After the collapse of Rome, much technology was lost along with knowledge of the past. The ruins of Bath became the work of giants, Stonehenge their temple and long barrows their graves. Only lightly converted to Christianity, people knew that their ancestors had worshipped other gods, had perhaps been descended from those huge gods, mountain-crushers, sea-drinkers.

The half-forgotten gods were regarded as devils by the new Christian Church, which took every opportunity to vilify them. Eventually old gods, ancestors and the Devil became gloriously confused. This explains why there is sometimes uncertainty in European folk tales as to whether the villain of a story is a giant or the Devil (*See* The Devil's Arrows).

As folk tales get closer to our own time, belief in real giants waned. No longer terrifying, they seem to become increasingly stupid; often tricked, as in 'Jack the Giant Killer', by the sort of thing a baby would see straight through. However, the four Yorkshire giants in this chapter are still powerful: one is a kind road-builder and three are, let's face it, pretty seriously nasty.

# The Giant of Dalton Mill

## Western Moors

Jack was a lad full of mischief. He skived off any work whenever he could, not because he was lazy exactly, but because he was more interested in the things going on around him. He loved to wander the wild moorland at Pilmore near Topcliffe where he lived. There he collected birds' eggs and set snares for rabbits, as was commonly done by lads in those days, but as well as eking out the family's food, he also liked to watch things. There was plenty to entertain him: not just dragonflies, tadpoles or frogs, but deer, foxes and badgers as well.

One day he was lying on his front peering into a pool when a huge shadow fell across him. He looked up: it was a giant, a very big giant with only one eye.

Jack immediately knew who he was; everyone did. His mother had warned him only that morning, 'Don't go on the moor, Jack, or the giant of Dalton Mill might get you!' He had, naturally, ignored her. Now he was realising, too late, that not everything your mother tells you is rubbish.

The giant reached down and picked up Jack as easily as if he had been a stick. Jack kicked, struggled and shouted, but, of course, no one came to help him.

The giant carried him up hill and down dale until they came to the mill. Dalton Mill has been rebuilt several times over the years, but when the giant lived there, it was a terrible place. You could smell it from miles away, and when you got closer clouds of flies would rise up, buzzing, from its gloomy walls. You see, the giant did not mill wheat – he ground human bones. Every couple of days he went off hunting for people, dragged them back to his mill, butchered them and then ground their bones into flour. The meat he would either cook into a nasty stew, or just eat raw and dripping. The bone flour he would mix with blood and bake into loaves of bread. They were a bit on the heavy side but the giant enjoyed them. After dinner, he would lie on the floor or in his chair by the fire and sleep, his big knife clasped firmly in his hand.

Jack thought that he was going to die as the giant strode up to his horrible mill. He was carried through the door and thrown carelessly onto the bloodstained floor. He waited, frozen with terror, for the giant to get out his famous knife, long as a scythe blade, so people said – but to his surprise the giant bent awkwardly down to him, and said 'I'll not eat tha if thoo'l work for me.'

It seems that the giant was getting old and a bit rheumaticky. He found it hard to do all the things that a mill requires to keep working properly; cogs need oiling and grindstones need dressing – especially when you use them to grind bones!

Jack grabbed the chance of survival with both hands, even if it meant that he was now the giant's prisoner. There was only one door to the mill, which the giant always carefully locked when he went out.

He began to learn something of the miller's art whether he wanted to or not: there was absolutely nothing else to do and he knew better than to ignore the giant's instructions. He also learned to make himself scarce and put his fingers in his ears when the giant brought his victims home.

What did he eat? Don't ask!

The giant had a truly nasty dog called Truncheon, who was a smelly, scurvy- and flea-ridden snappy dog who delighted in making Jack's life a misery, nipping his ankles and lifting its leg on him when he was sleeping. Jack did not dare do anything to Truncheon in revenge, because the dog was the giant's best mate. Their eating habits were very similar; sometimes Jack felt quite sick hearing them both gobbling down their dinners, growling when one thought the other had got too close.

Seven months – or was it seven years? – went by. Jack worked for the giant, fettling the machinery, fetching and carrying, doing an occasional mop up. He kept looking for a chance of escape but he never found one. The giant slept very lightly and that one eye was always half open.

One day Jack was idly looking out of the window, feeling more than usually homesick and miserable. It was sunny and hot outside. The moors would be full of life, he thought, and here he was shut up away from everything. It must almost be time for Topcliffe Fair, he realised with a pang. He loved Topcliffe Fair.

That afternoon when the giant had eaten his dinner and was stretched out on the floor, his head on a sack, looking as relaxed as he ever did, Jack asked if he might go to Topcliffe Fair as he had not had a single day off yet.

'I'll come straight back afterwards,' he said, looking at the giant as innocently as he could.

The one eye opened with a snap. 'What sort of gobshite do you think I am?' he said.

So that was that.

'Right,' thought Jack to himself, 'this means war, thoo mean great naff-head, thoo vicious, ungrateful old – old –' but he couldn't think of a bad enough word.

Jack laid his plans – well, he would have if he could have thought of any plans to lay. The giant's eye followed him more often than ever now and when its owner was not around the horrible dog was always there, scratching and drooling and waiting to give him a nasty nip.

The weather grew hotter and the mill smellier. Jack watched the giant after dinner hoping that the warmth would make him sleep more deeply. Several times he managed to make it to the door before that big eye opened and looked around for him.

One baking hot afternoon, the giant did indeed fall into a deeper sleep than usual. As Jack watched, he saw the grasp on the terrible knife slacken. The huge fingers uncurled a little. Jack held his breath and gently eased the knife out of the giant's fist. He gripped its handle tightly and looked at the sleeping monster;

there was only one thing to do. Taking a deep breath Jack stabbed the knife with all his force into that one evil eye.

The giant uttered a terrible scream and, as Jack leapt away, he struggled to his feet fumbling with both hands at his wounded eye.

'I'm blind! I'm blind! That miserable little worm has blinded me! Get him, Truncheon!'

He lunged, shouting and swearing around the room, thrusting his hands here and there to catch Jack. 'I'll catch thoo! I'll squash thoo!' He threatened Jack with every terrible death he could think of – and they were many! Eventually he realised that he would never catch Jack that way, so he went to the door and stood with his back to it.

'I'll stand here while I brak thah neck! I will! I'll never rest! Thoo'll never get out!'

This was an unforeseen setback. Jack looked around. The horrible dog was barking and jumping about showing its yellow teeth, though it did not attack. (It was, basically, a coward.) Jack had a sudden idea – or perhaps he remembered an old tale his mother had once told him – he caught Truncheon by the scruff of the neck and, before the dog knew what he was doing, he had cut its throat with the giant's knife.

Then he skinned it.

It took time because his hands were shaking so much and because all the while the giant was moaning and howling so loudly he could hardly think. When the skin was ready, he pulled it over his head and back. He had left the head on and, supporting it with one hand, he crawled towards the giant, whining. He butted the giant's leg with the head and barked in quite a good imitation of Truncheon. The giant reached down a hand and felt the dog's head. Jack waggled it a bit and whined again.

'Tha's sorry for me, Truncheon. Good dog, faithful dog!' He patted the dog's back. (Jack was nearly knocked over!) Another urgent whine. 'Want to go out for a piss, does tha?'

Slowly the giant unfastened the great lock and slid back the huge bolts. The door swung open. Freedom! Jack scuttled out as

fast as his legs could carry him into the beautiful summer sunlight. Throwing off the dog's skin, he ran and ran and ran until he was safely back home.

Later that evening Jack, thoroughly washed and with his joyful parents, was to be seen at Topcliffe Fair telling his story to anyone who would listen.

'A likely tale!' some said, but others wondered if there might be some truth in it.

Time went by and nothing more was heard of the giant. No more unwary travellers or lonely shepherds disappeared. People began to think Jack's tale might be true, however unlikely. Soon a well-armed band of brave folk ventured to Dalton Mill. There, right in front of the door they found the giant, dead and covered with a veritable mountain of buzzing flies. Jack's blow had obviously done more damage than he had thought and pierced the giant's brain.

They buried the giant in front of his house – the big mound is still there. The knife was kept inside the mill and shown to visitors as proof of the story well into our own time.

Jack recovered quickly from his adventure. Thanks to his stay with the giant, he was so skilled in the miller's art that a few years later he actually got a job in that very trade (as far away from Dalton Mill as he could get), but to the end of his days he could never stand dogs!

## Wade and His Wife Bell

*Western Moors*

Not all giants are evil. Clumsy they may be but grinding bones for flour is a deviant practice pursued by only a very few – in Yorkshire, at any rate. Most Yorkshire giants employ themselves in changing the landscape or throwing stones about.

Wade and his wife Bell were both giants. He had once been a Germanic sea-god (related to Woden) famous for owning a magic boat, but he liked it so much in North Yorkshire that he decided to settle there with his wife and his son, Weyland. There not being many giants' houses available, they first had to build a nice castle to live in. Wade wanted to live at Mulgrave near Sandsend where he could keep an eye on his boat, but Bell wanted to live further west near the moors at Pickering, where there was better grazing for their giant cow. They argued about it for a while, but in the end they decided to build two castles and split their time between them.

They each began to build in their chosen place, lugging huge stones from the moors. However, they had only one giant hammer between them (human hammers were not nearly big enough of course), so they had to share it.

'WHERE'S THE HAMMER?' Wade would yell from his building site near the sea.

'COMING OVER!' Bell would scream back from Pickering, flinging it the eighteen odd miles to Mulgrave. And so they went on, throwing and catching the hammer as they needed it.

Eventually the two castles were built and the giants began to live in them, sometimes strolling by the sea at Sandsend; sometimes taking the air on the hills by Pickering.

The giant cow, Bell's pride and joy, wandered the moors wrapping her huge tongue around trees and bushes as she took each mouthful. Cows are notorious for 'poaching' the ground with their sharp feet. Bell's cow had gigantic hooves and when it rained her hoof prints filled with water, creating the bogs still found on the moors. Over time, these became deeper and more dangerous. Poor Bell, giantess though she was, grew tired of plodding through

marsh and mire to milk the cow each day. She often complained to Wade saying how much she wished there was a nice smooth road between Mulgrave and Pickering to make milking time easier. She said it so frequently that, like any husband, in the end Wade ran out of excuses for inaction.

'Alright,' he said. 'You get the stones and I'll lay them.'

Bell began to collect stones. She got some from the moors and some from the beaches off the East Coast, carrying them in her vast apron. Sometimes she picked ones that were too heavy to carry the whole distance to where Wade was working, so she had to drop them by the side of the path where they still lie today. At one place, her apron strings broke, dumping twenty cartloads of rocks at a place now called The Devil's Apronful.

Wade made the road's solid base out of big stones. Then he added a second layer of smaller ones well hammered down. Finally, he surfaced the whole thing with sand brought up from the seaside in Bell's capacious apron. Both the giants worked hard, despite the odd problem, and soon the beautiful new road stretched smoothly from Mulgrave to Pickering, across the most difficult parts of the moors. At last Bell was able to come and go from milking her cow without getting her boots full of mud.

However, just as the countryside never looks the same after the building of a motorway, so the moors now looked rather different. Apart from the great stones Bell had dropped all over the place, there was the new Hole of Horcum. This had been created when Wade got angry with Bell one day and scooped up a big handful of mud to throw at her – you can still see the marks of his fingers on the sides of the Hole. Being a giant he was naturally a bad shot, so the mud missed Bell and landed on the other side of the moors where it is now called Blakey Topping.

Their son had also added something to the landscape. They took him along with them when they were building the road and one day they accidentally left him behind at Sleights Moor. At first he was quite happy playing with some big boulders, but eventually he grew hungry. He could see his mother in the distance so he threw a boulder at her to try to get her attention.

It must have been a freak throw because on this occasion he did actually succeed in hitting her. As Bell was a giantess, the only thing that got hurt was the boulder, which bounced off and fell three miles away at Swart Hill with a big piece cracked off. There it stood until broken up about 200 years ago, ironically for road stone.

Once the road was finished, the giant family seems to have lived happily for the rest of their lives. Wade was buried at Mulgrave (or, some say, Goldsborough) where Wade Stones mark his enormous grave. The cow died too and one of its huge ribs used to be shown at Mulgrave Castle (though ignorant people say that it was just a whale's jawbone!).

After their death the road gradually fell into disuse. It became overgrown with grass, though local people never forgot where it was. Some posh university folk say that the road was originally built by the Romans, but in that case, why is it still known in North Yorkshire as Wade's Causeway?


## The Devil's Arrows

*Western Moors*

One day a priest of the new Christian religion was preaching to the local people in the open air near Aldborough. He was encouraging them to convert and leave their old evil gods behind. Suddenly a venerable Druid appeared among them, speaking fervently on behalf of the old religion. People began to listen to him with interest.

The priest, looking at the old Druid intently, noticed that his feet were in fact the cloven hooves of a goat and that furthermore they were melting the rock on which he was standing. ' Devil! I defy you!' he shouted, holding up the cross. The Devil – rather too easily discomforted, I think – flung off his disguise and ran away. However he now had stony boots where the rock had melted onto his feet, so when they had cooled sufficiently to allow them to be removed, he deposited them at Howe Hill – about six miles away.

Later he returned to the hill carrying three (originally four) giant arrows – or possibly thunder bolts – intending to take revenge on Aldborough town. Unfortunately he spoilt his awesome appearance by uttering the feeble doggerel, 'Borobrigg keep out o' t' way, For Aldboro town I'll ding down today!'

Aldborough needn't have worried: being a giant he missed it by miles. (Boroughbridge, on the other hand, only just escaped). Three of his impressive arrows remain standing just outside the town. The fourth was uprooted in a search for treasure and then used as the foundation of a bridge over the River Test.

# THE GIANT OF PEN HILL

*Wensleydale*

What happens to gods when their cult dies? Someone once said that the gods of the old regime become the demons of the new, but there is an alternative: sometimes they shrink, retire to the country and sink comfortably into some borrowed local story.

Perhaps it was Thor who fathered the giant of Pen Hill. Left behind by the departing Vikings he might have become bitter and sullen; taken to keeping pigs to feed his voracious appetite; forgotten his friendship with humankind. Perhaps he fathered, on a passing frost giantess a son who inherited the worst characteristics of both, strong and fearless but cold as the rocks of Pen Hill.

Whatever the truth of his origin, to the inhabitants of Wensleydale the giant seemed to have always been there in his grim keep on top of Pen Hill, growing more evil with every passing year, a huge threatening presence, seldom seen but feared nevertheless, an ominous volcano on the edge of their peaceful fields.

Few ventured into the forest, with which a large part of Wensleydale was covered in those days. That was where the giant kept his swine, his one delight. You must not imagine that these pigs were like the naked pink deflated balloons you see lying about in the fields nowadays. No! These were wild pigs, covered, rather like the giant himself, with coarse tawny hair. They had long legs and ridged backs and could slip through the woods silently when they wished, searching for acorns and roots with their long sensitive snouts. They were huge and vicious, both the boars and the sows, with crushing jaws and wickedly curved tusks. From time to time they came into the peasants' fields and devastated their crops, but no one dared object, or even try to drive them off, for if there was one thing that the giant could not stand it was people interfering with his swine.

To assist him with herding these pigs the giant had a great boarhound, Wolfhead, his only friend. The swine obeyed him as they would obey no other dog and he drove them wherever his master wished, or hunted for strays deep in the forest. Even the fierce boars who defended the herd, huge battering rams of sinew and muscle, avoided him.

Wolfhead was descended on his father's side from the terrible Fenris Wolf, feared and bound by the Norse gods. It was from him that he had inherited his fierceness. From his mother, however, he had inherited the faithfulness of dogkind and all that faithfulness was devoted to the giant. During the day he worked hard for his master. In the evening he dozed with the giant by the fire, drooling on his master's boots but always alert for the rare pat or kind word.

Every morning Wolfhead drove all of the swine past the giant, two by two; first the red-eyed boars, then the sows and lastly the little squealing striped piglets. The giant delighted in his fierce way to see his pigs paraded daily before him. He liked to count their increasing numbers and check their fatness, for, of course, all his darlings ended their days on his plate.

One day Wolfhead and his master were walking through the meadows by the River Ure when they came upon a flock of sheep. Wolfhead trembled with excitement, but he kept his eyes on his master. The giant smiled evilly. 'Go on, lad, enjoy yourself!' he said.

The hound bounded forward. The sheep turned and ran, bleating pitifully. He leapt upon one and tore its throat out with a single jerk of his powerful head. The taste of blood drove him to frenzy and in a moment, he had killed three more and was gambolling down the field in pursuit of a fourth. This was fun!

'Stop him! Stop him!'

There was a young woman running across the meadow towards the giant. 'Please! Call your dog off! These are our sheep!'

The giant turned his great shaggy head towards the sound of the voice and stared at the person who had the effrontery to interfere. She stopped at a safe distance, wringing her hands in a mixture of grief and impotent anger.

'Call your dog off, for pity's sake, Master!'

The giant began to laugh. Wolfhead swung around to check that what he was doing still had his master's approval. He need not have worried.

'Go on, Wolfhead! Get the rest of the woolly bleaters!'

The girl made as though to run to their aid, but she did not dare. Tears poured down her cheeks as she watched the destruction of her flock.

The giant had no experience of women; he lived alone with only the dog and an old male servant for company. The sight of a weeping woman made him feel uncomfortable and confused. He did not like it. Or did he? He could see that her hair was as pale as the soft fur on Wolfhead's belly, and her cheeks were as pink as the snout of a newborn piglet. He supposed that meant she was pretty. Pretty was good. In an instant, he was in love.

Giants are not noted for their romantic courting. Pursuit and rape are more their line and this giant was no exception. In two steps, he was close to the girl and he began to stroke her hair and fondle her. She shrank back in horror, pushing his huge hands away before she turned away and ran as fast as she could.

The giant followed, but in her bare feet she easily outdistanced him. Growing angry, he called to Wolfhead. 'Get me that girl!'

Wolfhead gave the sheep he had just killed one last bite and did as his master wished. His heavy paws thudded over the meadow; he began baying, blood dripping from his jaws. The girl had nearly reached the edge of the forest when she turned her head to see how close her pursuer was and missed her footing. She fell heavily, winding herself. As Wolfhead leapt up to her, she seized the only thing that came to hand, a sharp rock, and struck him on the nose with all her force.

Wolfhead staggered back with a howl and began to paw at his nose. The girl tried to struggle to her feet, gasping for breath but before she could rise the giant was standing over her, his face full of fury. 'Hurt my hound will you?' he snarled, 'There's for you then, you bitch!' and he struck her again and again with his cudgel until she moved no more.

When the shepherd found his devastated flock and the broken body of his daughter, his grief was too deep for tears. He did not need to ask who the perpetrator was for the giant's footprints were all around crushing the sweet meadow grass. He let out a terrible cry that echoed off the sides of Pen Hill and brought the peasants working nearby to his side. The giant, on his way home, heard it too and laughed gleefully.

Hatred of the giant now spread along the valley as never before. It flowed down the banks of the Ure on the tongues of herdsmen and grew hot in secret by a hundred hearth-fires as people remembered his wrongs.

One morning in the autumn of that year, the giant noticed that as the swine trotted past him two by two there was one young boar on its own. A boar was missing.

'Wolfhead!' shouted the giant, kicking him viciously. 'You're getting old and lazy. You've lost a boar! Go and find it, or by Thor I'll kick your ribs into kindling! Take that as a reminder!'

Wolfhead slunk away into the forest while the giant walked impatiently up and down, counting and recounting his swine. It was noon before he heard Wolfhead's baying and ran following the sound, to a glade in the wood. There lay the body of one of his most promising young boars, pierced through the heart by an arrow.

The volcano of the giant's anger poured out. He beat down bushes and trees. He roared so loudly that birds fell out of their nests and people as far away as Hawes stuck their fingers in their ears. Wolfhead, remembering the kicks, crept away on his belly and hid deep in the forest.

When the giant had recovered a little, he flung the dead boar over his shoulder and crashed off home. Seizing the old man, his only servant, by the neck he ordered him to go to the people of Wensleydale and tell them that the Lord of the Dale (he meant himself) commanded that all men who could bear a bow should present themselves at the old meeting-place on the cliff of Pen Hill in a month's time.

'Is it for a war?' wavered the old man, who knew nothing of the death of the boar. 'Aye, a war of a sort! Tell them that!' said the giant. 'And tell them also what will happen to them if they fail to turn up. Be inventive!'

That evening, as the giant sat gloomily by the fire, he realised that something was missing. Wolfhead was not there, thumping his tail and looking fondly up into his master's face. He went to stand at the door of his keep and scanned the forest below. 'Wolfhead!' he roared. 'Come here this instant!'

There was a slight rustling of the bushes at the edge of the forest. The giant looked closer and saw that Wolfhead was crouching there, cowering. He whistled but the dog did not move. 'Damn your hide, come here!' Wolfhead stayed where he was.

The giant's cudgel was, as usual, in his hand. In a moment of fury, he threw it with all his might, and in a second, the only friend he had ever had was dead.

The month given to the peasants was up. The following day was set for the meeting. The old servant had returned exhausted. He saw that Wolfhead was no longer around, but he did not dare ask questions. He guessed that the hound was dead when the swine no longer appeared two by two in the morning. His master sat by the fire muttering darkly to himself, 'He asked for it! Disobey me and die!'

The old servant trembled for the fate of the men of Wensleydale.

Perhaps there were some wise peasants who did not obey the giant's summons, but they were few and far between. The meeting place at the cliff on Pen Hill was filled with men, from old grandsires to half-grown boys. They had all brought their bows as requested and no doubt would have been pleased to use them on the giant if only they had had a brave enough leader, but the fear for their families kept them all cowards.

The giant stood huge and threatening on the brow of the hill. He surveyed the gathering with a sneer. In his hand was an arrow. He held it up.

'You see this?' he said. 'What is it?' There was a stunned silence. The answer was so obvious that no one knew what to say. They suspected a trap.

'What is it, you curs?'

One brave man put his hand up. 'It's an arrow, Master.'

'Well done, you old fool! Yes, it's an arrow. The question is: who does it belong to?'

The peasants looked at one another. If they knew, they were not saying.

'I ask because I found it – in the heart of ONE OF MY BOARS! Give up the bowman or beware my wrath! I'm only going to ask you once!'

A little ripple of movement ran over the assembled men, but still they said nothing.

The giant stared at them for a moment, his face reddening with anger. Who did these slaves think they were? First the girl, then the dog, now this! He was the son of Thor the Thunderer! He would have blood for their disobedience!

'Very well, if that's the game you wish to play. You won't tell me now while your children live, so perhaps you will tell me when they're dying! Every man must come back here tomorrow bringing with him his youngest child. One child each or I kill all of you! Think about it tonight. Now GO!'

Shaken and sullen, the men turned and retreated down the hill. As they went they passed an old beggar man standing beside the path. He wore a ragged grey cloak and leaned on a staff. His hat was pulled down on one side to hide a missing eye. He nodded at the passing peasants but they were too humiliated to respond or meet his piercing gaze.

'Who is that man?' the giant asked his servant.

'I don't know his name, my lord. I've seen him around from time to time in the Dale, but never spoken to him.'

'He has an insolent look. Tell him to take himself off!' As the giant spoke, the old man stirred and moved towards him.

'What do you want?' the giant demanded.

'To get a good look at you,' replied the old man offensively.

The giant could see no fear in the one flashing eye that gazed sideways up at him. It made him uneasy.

'Well, now you've seen me, so you can take your dirty carcass off.'

'What do you intend to do to the children?'

'That's for me to know and those filth to find out!'

'It's Thor's Day tomorrow.'

'What do I care? Thor was my father.'

'He killed warriors and monsters, not children.'

'How do you know what the great god Thor did, old greybeard?'

'That's for me to know and you to find out.'

Suddenly the old man struck the ground with his staff. The blow did not seem hard and yet the rocks rang and the stone keep shuddered. The astonished giant took a step backwards. The old

man laughed as he turned away, and the giant and his servant heard him say, almost to himself, 'Be warned: you stand on the brink!' He strode swiftly away down the winding path into the Dale but his last words came floating up, 'One more step and you fall!'

The next morning the giant's old servant was emptying the slop pail outside the kitchen when he heard a deep croaking. Looking up he saw two huge ravens circling the keep. Round and round they went until the servant was giddy. He was filled with fear, for he thought he knew whose ravens they were; he rushed to tell the giant. His master once more sat by the fire, muttering. The servant recognised the warning signs and he hovered uncertainly.

'What is it?' growled the giant. 'Speak up man, don't stand there gibbering!'

'Ravens, Master. Ravens flying around the keep –'

'Ravens? What do I care for ravens, you idiot?'

'It's a warning! Surely you know –'

'A warning! I'll give you warning, you idiot!' and he aimed a vicious kick at the old servant that felled him to the ground. The giant kicked him again and again until he was tired.

'Are you dead yet?' he yelled, but there was no reply. The giant spat on the body and, picking up his great cudgel, marched out to await the men of Wensleydale and their children.

But the old servant was not dead. He was badly hurt, but he knew what to do next. He hauled himself to his feet and slowly staggered out to the shed, where the wood and peat for lighting the fire was stored.

'I've seen your ravens, my lord,' he said to the sky. 'I know you are with us!' Then he began to fill baskets with peat. Nine baskets he filled and began, painfully, to drag them into the keep.

The giant had not walked more than a hundred yards from his keep when he noticed something reddish lying across his path. He was filled with an unfamiliar sense of foreboding. As he got closer, he saw nine of his great boars lying dead across the path.

A hundred yards further on there was another nine – and a little further yet, another.

The giant ran now like a wild elephant, so furious that he foamed at the mouth, striking at everything he met with his cudgel. The huge veins in his neck and forehead stood out like hawsers, 'By Thor! I shall kill every one of them! Smash their heads, beat their bones to flour, pull down their houses, and crush their wives and children! Wensleydale will become a desert!'

The men of Wensleydale stood at the meeting place near the cliff, holding their young children in their arms. The children were afraid and many were crying.

As the sound of the giant's violent approach reached them they all trembled and some turned to flee, no matter what might happen to them. Suddenly the old man in the grey cloak stood before them. No one had seen him come and yet he was there, not exactly smiling but somehow comforting. Even the most fearful seemed to gain courage from his presence.

As the giant appeared over the crest of the hill, he looked so powerful that no one thought he could be prevented from killing them all. Then the old man stepped forward and held up his staff – or was it now a spear? The giant stopped as dead as if he had run into a wall. Still he waved his cudgel.

'I know you, Lord of the Gallows!' he panted. 'And I defy you!' The watchers thought that he would strike the old man down but at that very moment two ravens appeared as though from thin air and flew close over his head. 'Look!' said the old man, pointing towards the hilltop behind the giant. He swung around and all of them could see a tall plume of black smoke mixed with roaring pillars of flame rising from the direction of the giant's keep.

'I did warn you!' said the old man. He made a small gesture with his hands and the giant's cudgel splintered and fell to the ground. The giant did not seem to notice, for his eyes were now fixed on something else, something that made them wide with horror. His mighty limbs began to tremble and his mouth fell open. He tried to speak, but could not utter a sound. To the astonishment of all the men of Wensleydale their enemy began to stumble backwards his hands raised as though to protect himself.

Silhouetted against the smoke and fire, two figures were approaching. One was a girl, pale and slender, the other a great boarhound. Their eyes glittered and though they seemed solid enough their feet did not touch the ground. The girl held the boarhound on a leash, but his jaws slavered and his limbs strained as he tried to get at his former master. Back and back the giant staggered until he stood at the very edge of the cliff. Then, nodding briefly to the old man, the shepherd's daughter loosed the hound. With one spring, Wolfhead leapt at the giant's throat. Dog and giant went backwards over the cliff together.

# 3

# DRAGONS

## ON DRAGONS

A fine clutch of eggs, probably laid by dragons from Scandinavian stories brought over by the Vikings, hatched out in North Yorkshire. The hatchlings settled across the county: Sockburn, Handale, Loschy Wood, Slingsby and Sexhow all have tales of dragons and their inevitable destruction by a variety of heroes. Unfortunately, the stories are so similar that one or two are quite enough.

All the dragons appear to have been of a similar type – the sort that coils around a hill, snakelike with poisonous breath, rather than the fire-drakes found further south. (*See* Ragnar Lodbrok and the Founding of York for an early version.) Only one, the Sockburn dragon, could fly. One, the Loschy Hill dragon, whose story is given below, could heal itself by rolling on the ground (a feature borrowed from the Greek legend of Alcyoneus and Heracles). The Sexhow dragon had its skin nailed to the church door whence it was supposedly removed by that man-turned-myth, Oliver Cromwell.

Their diet varied. Some just ate local people, some liked the daily milk of nine cows; one, fussy but a little conventional, preferred virgins.

As for their killers, most go on to marry rich heiresses once they have removed the dragon; however, two heroes and their dogs are tragically killed by their dragon's poisonous breath, though only after the dragon is safely dead.

One dragon appears to be connected with establishing land tenure. It involved such a weird ceremony that I cannot resist including it briefly here.

# THE SOCKBURN DRAGON

*Northern Moors*

The manor of Sockburn, which lies just over the River Tees, had a troublesome dragon. Sir John Conyers was the hero ready to fight it. The Bowes Manuscript in the British Museum states that:

> The scent of the poyson was soe strong that noe person was able to abide it, yet hee by the providence of God overthrew it and lyes buried at Sockburn before the Conquest, but before hee did enterprise it (having but one child) he went to the churche in compleate armour and offerd up his sonne to the Holy Ghost, which monument is yet to see and the place where the serpent lay is called Gray Stone.

The manor was owned by the Bishop of Durham and each time a new bishop was appointed whichever descendent of Conyers was alive at the time had to meet him in the middle of the bridge over the Tees and offer him an ancient sword with the following words:

> My Lord Bishop. I hereby present you with the falchion wherewith the champion Conyers slew the worm, dragon or fiery flying serpent which destroyed man, woman and child; in memory of which the king then reigning gave him the manor of Sockburn, to hold by this tenure, that upon the first entrance of every bishop into the county the falchion should be presented.

The falchion (a thirteenth-century one that is now in Durham Cathedral), was then handed back. This tradition continued to be kept until the early nineteenth century (though it is possible there was a revival once in the 1920s).

## THE LOSCHY HILL DRAGON

### Hambledon Hills

On Loschy Hill, above Stonegrave near Nunnington, there once lived a dragon. It was one of the poisonous kind, more like a snake than a winged firedrake. It dribbled poison across the land, breathing out plague and pestilence that killed man and beast. Fear spread over the whole area.

During the day, it lay dozing, entwined in the trees of Loschy Wood, or curled around the hill itself. Then a young man might, dared by his friends, climb the hill a little way and, if he were brave enough and undaunted by the poisonous fumes, gaze with fear on the vomit-yellow coil of its hideous body. At night, though, it would rouse itself and, slithering on the slime trail of its own poison, set out to hunt. Benighted travellers or straying beasts might see wisps of a white vapour flowing around them and be filled with a strange weakness, before the dragon took them into its deadly embrace and the razor-sharp teeth struck.

As it grew larger, its hunger grew greater. Soon whole flocks of sheep began to disappear, or a farmer would find his byre empty of cattle and nothing left but a trail of blackened and shrivelled grass across the field. A travelling 'reddleman' or tinker might arrive at the isolated farmhouse where he had been welcomed many a time before to find silence and dead dogs and a gruesome smell.

But how to get rid of such a monster? At first, bands of irate farmers and peasants tried to drive the dragon out with flails and pitchforks. Many died in a few minutes. Those that were left, tried to burn the wood, but although the dragon had no fire of its own, it was of dragon-kind and what dragon ever feared fire?

Next the knights began to come. They were better protected against the creature's poison with their closed helms and steel armour, but the dragon merely killed their horses and crushed the life out of their riders before they could use their swords.

People began to despair.

Then Sir Peter Loschy, a knight whose lands were in nearby Nunnington returned from many years on crusade. He had hardly dismounted before his servants were telling him about the terrible dragon that had settled so near his lands.

Now, Sir Peter was valiant, but he added a keen intelligence to his valour; he saw immediately that the usual approach to the dragon was doomed to failure. He had always been interested in blacksmithing – most knights were – and had spent many hours as a young man talking to his father's blacksmith and armourer, or watching him turning hard iron into shining armour. The day after his return, he went down to the smithy to chat to his old friend whose son now did most of the work. They talked about the dragon.

'Trouble is,' said the blacksmith, 'no armour is strong enough to withstand the crushing hug of the beast. It's as strong as a mill wheel and so fast that you're dead before you can get in a decent blow.'

'Brute strength is no good,' said the son, 'it's far stronger even than you, my lord!'

Sir Peter thought for a moment. 'If it's so strong,' he said, 'perhaps there's a way to use its strength against it. It doesn't seem to have any of the usual weak spots.'

'Suppose,' said the son, thoughtfully, 'just suppose that you could use its own strength to kill it by making it drive itself onto your sword.'

'Or,' broke in the smith, getting a little excited now, 'suppose you wore a band of sharp spikes around your waist. Then when it tightened its coils …'

'Or better still,' shouted Sir Peter. 'suppose I had knives –'

'– Sticking out!' added the blacksmith.

'All over your armour!' finished the son. They looked at each other.

'That's it!' they choroused.

Making the spiked armour was not an easy task. It had to be

carefully designed and made so that the spikes did not break off under pressure. The three spent long evening hours together, drawing plans and occasionally shouting at each other. Finally, the design was finished and the blacksmith and his son set about making it. Neighbours came around to complain that the continual clinking and clanking of hammers kept them awake at night, but when they were told the reason for the noise, they bit their lips and went home.

At last all was ready and Sir Peter, looking a little like an armoured hedgehog, set off for the dragon's hill on foot (for he did not wish to risk his warhorse), and accompanied only by his dog, Tip.

It was just as well Sir Peter was fit, for it was a steep climb in all that steel, but at last he began to hear a sound that chilled his blood, brave though he was: the sound of breaking branches and a low deep hiss as if the very ground were hissing. Tip began barking, and, before Peter even caught a glimpse of what was coming, the dragon, which had been sleeping in the trees above him, dropped its coils over his head. He was completely wrapped in the hideous, writhing, yellow body for a moment and then, as the coils drew together for the final squeeze, a shudder ran through them. A terrible howling came from dragon's mouth as it stabbed itself on the countless razor-sharp knives of Sir Peter's armour. Swiftly it released him, twisting and curling and bleeding as it slipped away. In an instant, Peter was pursuing it, sword in hand, striking as hard as he could. The sword bit deep into the flesh and the howling redoubled. The dragon was badly hurt, but not yet beaten, and as Peter leapt after it, it turned and reared up like a great cobra to strike down this impudent dinner. This time Peter was faster and, with a mighty two-handed double stroke, he cut through its neck and saw the horrible head bounce on the ground and roll away. The body thrashed about on its own, smashing small trees, but Peter, sure that he had finally rid the land of the monster, leaned on his sword to get his breath. Not for long! As he watched, the head rolled back across the grass and with a sort of a leap joined itself onto its body again. In an instant, before Sir Peter's horrified eyes, the dragon was once more reared up snarling and prepared to strike.

Now Peter had a true fight on his hands. Again and again he cut the dragon into collops, only to see, again and again, the severed

parts roll on the earth and then join up again. Now the knight was getting very tired. Fear gnawed at him. His tired brain could only think of one thing: how to stop the pieces of dragon joining together. His situation was getting desperate when he had a sudden flash of inspiration. He whistled for Tip, who, like any sensible dog, had stayed out of a battle too great for him, but who had showed his support by barking.

'Take it away!' Peter shouted, hitting a section of dragon towards Tip with his sword. Tip got the idea immediately and leapt forwards, seizing the bloody chunk. He raced off towards Nunnington and dropped it on holy ground near the church, then raced back to his master. It was a slow business, whittling the dragon down piece by piece. Both man and monster grew weaker, but still they tried to kill each other with all their remaining strength. Tip himself grew tired, dragging the heavy lumps all the way to Nunnington.

At last, the head alone was left. Tip wearily took the great thing with its dimming eyes and protruding tongue, and dragged it slowly away.

Sir Peter tore off his helm and sat down on the bloodstained ground. He was so tired he could scarcely lift his head. He was nearly asleep when, after a long time, Tip returned.

'We did it together!' said Sir Peter. 'Come here Tip, you good dog, you faithful dog!' Tip came up to him, tail wagging. He enthusiastically licked Sir Peter's face as his master gently patted his head.

But what was this? Suddenly Sir Peter began to cough, to choke and clutch at his throat. He looked down at Tip's mouth still red with the blood from the dragon's tongue, the dragon's poisonous tongue!

'Oh Tip!' he gasped. 'You have killed us!'

Swiftly the dragon's poison poured through his veins like an icy river; the last thing he saw in this world was his faithful dog, also falling … the dragon's last victim.

In Nunnington church there is a worn effigy of an unknown knight lying peacefully, his feet resting on his faithful dog. Ancient tradition says that this is the burial place of Sir Peter Loschy and the loving dog that unknowingly killed his master.

# 4

# CREATURES
# OF THE NIGHT

Granny sits in the inglenook of the fire with the cat in her lap. All around her snuggle her grandchildren on their little stools, warming their hands on evening bowls of bread and hot milk. It is Halloween and they want scary stories.

Sarah, the eldest, finishes her supper and puts down her bowl. 'Granny, why don't you tell us about the creatures of the night?' Granny pretends she can't remember. 'Yes you can,' Sarah persists. 'You know a list of them. It starts with Incubus, then there's Suck – Suck –'

'Succubus. You don't need to know about those – not yet anyway!'

'What else?'

'Nightmare – surely you don't want to hear any more.'

'Yes we do! Go on!'

Granny puts on her serious face. 'Well, alright then. I suppose it can't do any harm to warn you. There's Grim, Kirkgrim, Padfoot, Bogle, Gytrash and the worst of all …' The children wait in delicious suspense, though they know the answer. 'Bargest!'

'Tell us about Bargest, Granny!' whispers the smallest, milk dripping off her spoon .

'Yes!' shout the boys. 'Why is Bargest the worst?'

'Well –' Granny keeps them waiting, lighting her old pipe with a burning stick. She puffs for a while but the children know better than to hurry her now. 'It's the worst because …' Puff, puff, puff.

'Yes?'

'DEATH FOLLOWS IT!'

Gasps, not all pretended, from the group. Granny nods grimly, but Tom, the clever clogs, has to put his oar in. 'You don't always die when you meet it thought, do you? What about that feller from …'

'Oh, so you're the expert now, are you? Well, those who've actually been listening will recall that I said "death *follows* it", not "you die if you see it" – though …' adds Granny in her most sinister voice, 'that happens often enough. No, Bargest is a warning of death, either to you or someone you know, someone dear to you!'

'Is there one round here?' wavers little Sophie.

'No, honey,' Granny says quickly. 'It's found in lonely places, like moors or empty crossroads. You'll never see one round here. Our farm dogs 'ud get it, wouldn't they?' The boys are clearly disappointed by this.

'I'd like to see one, anyway,' says Jack stoutly. 'I'd put it on a string and bring it home to eat Sophie!' More shrieks and a few tears this time. Sarah slaps Jack and comforts Sophie. Granny lets her get on with it. She stares into the fire, puffing away at her pipe.

When peace is restored, however, she fixes Jack with a piercing eye, 'Well Jack, my clever lad, and how would you go about looking for Bargest? It can take any shape it pleases, you know. A dog, often, but also a horse, or a cow, a calf or even a cat like Tabby here,' She strokes the cat in her lap. 'You might see an old cat coming along the road one night and think it was Tabby until –'

'Until what?' the older children encourage hopefully. Sophie buries her face in Sarah's skirt.

'Then you'd notice its eyes!'

'What about its eyes, Granny?'

'They're big, horrible, huge! Like the dog in the story with the eyes as big as saucers. But they're not like the eyes of a right beast. Oh no, not they. They're like rings of brilliant colour, like a

Catherine wheel. Then you'd know it wasn't a cat, but then it would be too late!'

The children consider this interesting piece of animal physiology. 'And does it make a noise?' asks Paul.

'Oh, there's a terrible howling shriek when it catches its prey, but normally you'll never hear it creep up behind you because its feet,' she drops her voice to a whisper, 'make no noise!'

'No noise. Even when it's a horse?'

'Absolutely no noise. Its feet are as quiet as Tabby's. The only sound you'll ever hear comes when it's very close to you. Just imagine, you're coming home along the road one night and get a funny feeling that something is following you. You look around but you can't see anything in the darkness. You go on a while but sooner or later …'

'What?'

'You'll hear,' Puff, puff, 'a strange clinking-clanking noise.'

'Like a harness chain?'

'No, like a chain in a dungeon, a great big heavy chain. Bargest has one around its neck!'

'What do we do if we hear it?'

Granny looks around at them all. They stare back expectantly but at that very moment there comes a muffled sound of clinking – or is it clanking? – a chain! The children gasp. Granny gets to her feet (dropping Tabby, hissing, to the floor). She clutches her heart dramatically and points with a shaking finger into the darkness of the room behind the children. 'YOU RUN!' she shouts at the top of her voice. 'RUN FOR YOUR LIVES!' And all the boys do just that, rushing for the stairs or the back door.

'That got 'em!' says Granny, sitting down again. She knocks the ashes of the pipe out on the fender. Tabby jumps back up instantly. Sophie and Sarah, who, strangely, have not run away, are smiling and giggling a little.

'Good work, Sophie!' says Granny. 'What was it Sarah gave you?'

'Gyp's old chain!' Sophie holds up the dog-chain she has been hiding behind her back.

'So, when will you tell us about the Gytrash?' she asks.

# THE BARGEST OF TROLLER'S GILL

*Wharfedale*

There was once a foolish man called Troller who decided that he wanted to see the bargest, though all his friends warned him against it.

He decided to wait at a place it was known to inhabit, a dark gill between rocky cliffs where the Skyreholme Beck pours through a narrow channel before joining the Wharfe. No sane man would dare it at night, for though the fissure is very narrow, the gorge that the water has cut is very deep; any false step would mean death. The roar of the water in winter is deafening, the thunder of it resounding throughout one's whole body.

Troller would not be deterred. He dabbled in magic and believed that he had a charm that would protect him from the bargest while allowing him to defy and perhaps even control it, like a magician of old. He was obsessed with the idea, drawn to the horror and convinced that he was the hero who would bend the creature to his will.

He rose from his bed at midnight and, armed only with a small ash twig, set off in the moonlight for the gill. The deep sound of rushing water beneath him did not daunt him. He felt only excitement as he reached a twisted old yew tree at the edge of the gill and knelt beneath it. With the ash twig he drew a circle around himself in the earth, turned himself clockwise three times, knelt and kissed the ground three times. Now, he believed he was safe, fool that he was, and settled down to wait.

On a nearby hill there was a shepherd camping out with his sheep to protect the newborn lambs against predators. It was he who caught sight of what happened next and later told the tale in Skyreholme village. His attention was first drawn to the gill by the sound of Troller's voice calling out a challenge to the bargest.

'Come and meet me, Bargest, if you dare!'

Curious, but glad he was no closer; the shepherd peered towards the beck. He saw a spectral green light that began to glow along the gill illuminating the rocks. As it grew brighter, it was accompanied by the ominous sound of a clanking chain, which swiftly became louder and closer. There was a sudden rush and clatter of falling stones. The shepherd's blood ran cold as terrible shrieks burst without warning from the depths of the gill – whether those of a man or a beast he could not tell. They came again and again, dying away at last in a rattling howl that echoed across the moors. The shepherd and his dog waited, unable to move from fear, but they heard no more. The ghastly light died away and the beck flowed on undisturbed.

The shepherd was far too terrified to go and see what had happened. All night he huddled with his trembling sheepdog in the little lambing hut, unable to sleep, but the morning brought them more courage and they left the sheep and ventured down into the gill together. Almost immediately the dog began to bark.

Beneath the old yew tree lay Troller, his eyes open but unseeing, his face frozen in an expression of agonised terror. At first the confused shepherd thought that he must be wearing his red Sunday waistcoat, then he saw that terrible claws had torn open the poor man's chest. The remainder of his heart's blood was slowly trickling down into the beck.

From that night on, the place has been known as Troller's Gill.

# THE FELON SOW OF ROKEBY

## Northern Moors

Ralph de Rokeby had a problem: she was large and fierce and covered with rusty-red hair. She was a pig, a sow, a felon sow vicious beyond belief!

Sows can be aggressive when defending their piglets, but this sow had no piglets. What she did have is ripping eye-teeth and molars that could crush bone like a twig. Larger than three ordinary sows she ranged the side of the little River Greta like a warlord, attacking – and sometimes killing – anyone who came near her.

As the poem says: 'Was no barne that colde her byde.' (Meaning there was no man who could stand up to her.)

Baron Ralph did not know what to do with her; none of his men dared go near her so he could not kill her for food and he hesitated to try breeding from such a monster. In the end, the exasperated baron decided that he would give her away. There was a daughter house of Grey Friars in nearby Richmond and he knew that, being a begging order, it was always short of food. 'I'll give the cursed thing to them,' he thought. 'Kill two birds with one stone. Get rid of the sow and benefit my immortal soul at the same time!' He smiled wickedly.

The friars were overjoyed at the prospect of roast pork.

'There's just one thing,' the baron told them. 'You'll have to bring her home yourselves.'

Well, that was not a problem; they would just tie a rope to her leg and drive her home with a stick. 'Better take a couple of strong men with you,' suggested Baron Ralph carelessly, 'just in case.'

Friar Middleton was selected for this task and he picked two lay friary servants to help him, Pater Dale and Brian Metcalfe. The three men set off merrily with their rope and stick. They chatted of chitterlings and bacon, or stuffed chine and sausages.

They had no trouble at all finding the sow. There she was, lying under a tree by the River Greta. The three stopped abruptly.

'Holy Mother of God!'

They stared in amazement. 'Bacon for months, boys,' exclaimed Friar Middleton. 'Where's that rope?' Cautiously he began to approach the sow. She lifted up her head to watch him and very slowly got to her feet. Her muddy snout went snuffle, snuffle and her little red eyes peered at them from under her rusty eyebrows. She was about the size of a Shetland pony – but much more dangerous, as Friar Middleton discovered when she charged. Her trotters thundered over the ground. The three men turned and ran back into the wood, but the sow was much faster than any of them had expected and they had to hide behind trees. Their blood was up now, however; there was bacon at stake!

'We've got to get that rope on her leg!' shouted Friar Middleton. 'You two grab her round the neck and wrestle her to the ground while I tie the rope. Altogether now: one, two, three!'

It was not an heroic scene. The sow shook off Peter and Brian like drops of water and chased the friar into the river. When she turned back to deal with the others, Brian just managed to avoid being run down by shinning up a tree, and Peter was chased round and round cursing and shouting for help.

The men were determined not to give up; they regrouped and flung themselves at the pig. Friar Middleton leapt onto her back and had a short but exhilarating ride before being flung into a briar patch. Peter made the rope into a noose and tried to lasso the sow's head.

There was a lime kiln in the wood, used for burning chalk into lime for the fields. The sow avoided the noose and backed abruptly, managing to get her backside stuck in the entrance to the kiln.

'Quick! Get the rope on her!' Peter slipped the noose over her head.

'Got her!' The three shouted with triumph, punching the air.

Now that she was stuck, the sow seemed to quieten down. She stood panting, appearing beaten. The men took hold of the rope and began to haul. The sow's rear slowly became unstuck. As soon as she felt herself free, however, she suddenly leapt forward and attacked again, vicious jaws snapping. She took a lump out of Brian's calf and butted Peter violently into a thorn bush. When she turned her attention to Friar Middleton, he did not stop to fight but leapt up into a nearby sycamore tree with un-friarly agility.

They had reached a stand-off; one man clutching his bleeding leg; one gasping for breath; one sitting like an unwieldy grey bird in a tree; the felon sow strolled back and forth keeping watch on them all.

Now Friar Middleton began to grow angry at the sow's attitude. It was all very well for her to attack ordinary men like Peter and Brian, but he was a properly ordained friar and deserved more respect. He remembered how the birds fed St Cuthbert and how St Francis, the founder of his order, had preached to wild animals. She was an ignorant creature, he reflected, and would be improved by being instructed in the gospels. He slithered down the tree and, raising his hand in a dramatic gesture, he began to speak.

'What's he doing?' hissed Peter to Brian.

'I think he's preaching to the sow.'

'In Latin?'

'In Latin.'

'The sowe scho wolde not Latyne heare.' Recovering from what was no doubt surprise at her enemy's strange actions the pig squealed her rage and charged once more. Once more, the good friar had to take to his heels and flee to the wood.

When Baron Ralph saw his sow return home to her sty that evening, he noticed the rope hanging from her neck and knew that there had been a fight. He raised one eyebrow in amusement but said nothing. The sow settled down to sleep, well satisfied with her day.

It was a battered, scratched and miserable trio who stood before the warden of their friary attempting to explain why they had been defeated by a pig. Friar Middleton swore that she was not really a pig but the Devil in disguise.

The warden was not pleased with them, but neither was he going to give up. He settled down to write two letters. One was to the famous Gilbert Griffiths, a most renowned man-at-arms, and the other was to a well-known Spanish saracen-slayer. He begged them to go to Rokeby and slay the felon sow; a monster well worthy of their skill, he told them. In return, the friars would pray for their souls forever.

The two warriors could not resist the challenge and so the sow met her match at last – though vegetarians will be pleased to hear that she nearly managed to castrate the Spaniard before Gilbert felled her with his good sword. He took her back to Richmond cut in half and carried in two panniers strapped to a sturdy packhorse.

When the friars saw the pork arrive, their joy knew no bounds.

O how lustily they sang 'Te Deum' (We praise thee O God) before that night's dinner!

## THE GYTRASH

*Western Moors*

On the road from Egton Bridge to Goathland is a farmhouse called Julian Park. The land on which it is built was once, according to legend, the site of a castle built by an early member of the local de Mauley family. He was Julian de Mauley – and he was evil!

'Who is the fairest maid in Goathland?'

'It is Gytha, daughter of Gudron.'

'Bring her to me!' says Julian de Mauley.

'Sire, you have many women to please you. She is only a young virgin. Pease leave her be!'

'You fool!' says his master. 'I do not want her for that but to make this new castle of mine strong. The stones need a life to strengthen them!'

The servant leaps back in horror. 'Sire, the sacrifice of a cat or a dog will surely be sufficient to protect it. It would be evil beyond evil to kill a maid!'

'That evil I dare if it will make my castle impregnable.'

The people of Goathland weep and lament when they hear the news, but it is to no avail. De Mauley's men seize the girl.

'Who is the best mason in Goathland?'

'Sire it is Gudron, the father of Gytha.'

'Bring him here to me. None but he shall lay the stones that will shut his daughter in my wall.' But Gudron will not come. He swears that he will die before he kills his daughter in such a cruel way.

'I shall not kill you,' says Julian when Gudron is at last dragged before him. 'We shall see what torture will do!'

He hands Gudron over to his soldiers for torture. Gudron is a brave man. He holds out for a long time, but even the bravest may break in time. Weeping, he takes the trowel in his hand to enclose his beloved daughter in the castle wall.

She screams and weeps when they carry her to the place. She begs forgiveness for whatever harm she may have done to injure Julian (for she cannot understand his need).

'So pure! So sweet! Dear Gytha, you will guard my castle fittingly forever!'

Now the wall rises around her and the darkness with it. Her father tries with broken words to soothe her terror. Now only two stones remain to be laid. A loaf of bread, a jug of water, a spindle and wool are thrust mockingly through into the hole so that she will not waste her last hours. Gytha's blue eyes stare desperately into her father's for the last time as he shuts out her world forever.

The people of Goathland beg for her release while there is still time; they fall on their knees before Julian. Priests and monks warn him of holy vengeance for slaying the innocent. Julian laughs at them all, listening with impatience in the dark each night to the fading sound of Gytha's weak cries far inside his castle wall. At last they cease. Julian rejoices and orders a feast. Now his castle will be impregnable.

It is a year later. Julian lies asleep. Suddenly he awakes with a jump. There is a light in his room eminating from a drifting figure that moves slowly towards him. 'Who are you?' he cries, and then stops abruptly as he sees that the figure wears Gytha's dress and carries a spindle.

Her face, no longer beautiful, is emaciated, her shrivelled lips drawn back over her white teeth, but it is her eyes, her terrible blue eyes that make him understand that there is no escape. She drifts closer and holds her spindle over his feet. The thread of despair that she spun in her last days snakes down and binds together his feet and ankles, which lose all feeling, becoming cold and dead. Then she is gone. Next day he cannot stand or walk without a stick.

The following year, on the anniversary of her death, she returns and binds his legs with the thread that no one except Julian can see. Now he cannot ride his horse and must be carried on a chair.

And so it goes on year after year, each anniversary bringing a further loss of movement. It is like being slowly walled up. Julian consults doctors, priests and wise women. He covers himself with amulets and charms. He repents and confesses, and swears to do only good. He promises the people of Goathland freedoms they have only dreamed of if only they will pray for him. Maybe they do. But nothing works. On the tenth anniversary of Gytha's death, his servants find him dead and rigid in his bed. They had no cause to love him, but his death brings them no joy.

'He was cruel, living,' they say, 'God protect us against his spirit now he's dead!'

Their words prove prophetic. It is only a matter of months before the people of Goathland realise that Julian in death is indeed worse than he was in life. Labourers going home in the evening see it first: a huge demonic being in the shape of a giant black goat with fiery eyes and curving horns that spout flames. They run as fast as they can, but when they get home one of their number is missing.

'It's a gytrash!' whisper the old women. 'A gytrash in goat form. Who'd have thought we'd live to see such a thing in our time?'

'It's old Julian, if you ask me,' says the oldest man in the village. 'He's come back to destroy us one by one!'

'Why would he do that?' asked his little granddaughter from her stool at his side.

'He never loved the living, and we wouldn't pray for him. Now he's dead he hates us still more.'

Now all the villagers are filled with fear. No one dares stray away from home when it gets dark. Children, women and the old are kept indoors, for only the fastest runners can escape the gytrash if they meet it. Even so, many die.

Around the anniversary of Julian's death, something else begins to haunt the village as well. This time only young maidens are attacked. It is tall and pale, weeping constantly and carrying a spindle in its thin hand. It comes to the girls at night and wraps the wool from its spindle around their chests so that in a few weeks they sicken and die. 'Gytha blames us for not protecting her!' the mothers weep.

'Who will free us from these curses?' people ask each other. 'Our young folk seem doomed!' They pray and they ring the church bells to drive off evil, but nothing stops the ravages of the two spirits. The little granddaughter falls ill. Her grandfather calls a meeting of villagers.

'There is only one person who can help us,' he says. 'We have tried the holy ways, now we must try the unholy ones! Let us go and see the Spaewife of Fylingdales!'

The Spaewife is a witch, white, possibly, but many people fear her strange appearance and cryptic utterances. It is decided that the village elders will approach her. They take a suitable gift and cross the moor to her lonely hut.

After they have explained their problem, her sharp black eyes regard them silently from under her thick white hair. Then she says 'Tane to tither!' and shuts her door on them. Not another word do they get out of her.

The villagers discuss the possible meanings of these three words for days. Some think one thing and some another but no one agrees until the old grandfather suddenly understands. 'We should make t'ane fight t'ither!'

Now everyone can see it. Only a strong spirit like Gytha's can defeat the gytrash.

'But how do we get them to fight? Only the Spaewife knows anything about these creatures.' Back to see her they went.

The Spaewife is pleased that they have solved her riddle. She decides to help them further. 'Gytrashes are corpse-eaters, grave-haunters. Give gytrash a burial, he'll be there. Not churchyard, though. Killing Pits. An unbaptised bairn.'

The villagers look at each other in horror; they have no dead babies in the village and if they did, none would be unbaptised, but they dare not argue.

'What of Gytha?' asks the grandfather.

'The pale maid? She's gytrash's sworn enemy. Lure her with honey, fix her with wheat and salt. Then you'll see her come.'

They go home to lay their plans. As they have no real dead baby they make a corn-mell baby (a doll made from the last wheat sheaf at harvest), wrap it in a shawl and lay it in a little white coffin. The village sexton digs a deep grave at the Killing Pits (lumps and bumps of an ancient village a little way outside Goathland).

When the anniversary of the death of Gytha and Julian comes around again the villagers take honey and smear it here and there along the path from the castle to the Killing Pits. They strew grains of wheat and salt along the way as well. Then they wait for evening.

There is a solemn procession walking along the track to the Killing Pits. Hymns are being sung and a small white coffin is carried shoulder high. In its secret lair beneath the castle, the gytrash lifts its horrible head.

The procession reaches the grave and lowers the coffin into it. Prayers are said, though the ground is not consecrated, then the sexton fills in the hole. The mourners melt away, not back to the village but into hiding places in thickets and bushes round about. They wait.

Night closes down. The waning moon gives little light. Owls begin to hoot. A cold wind streams down from Julian Park towards the villagers and with it the distant gleam of flickering flames: the gytrash! Now its fiery eyes light up the path, the flames of its horns stream back over its shoulders. It keeps turning its head searching for the grave. It catches sight of the freshly turned earth and springs onto it. It begins to dig with hooves and horns. It is strong and fast. The waiting people begin to hold their breath. What if it realises it has been tricked before Gytha comes? They can hear its hooves grating on the little coffin. The church bells strike midnight.

But no! Another light is drifting down the road. The emaciated form of Gytha, enveloped in a greenish glow, floats past them towards the grave. The moment she sees the gytrash her blue eyes blaze and her skull-like face contorts as, no longer weeping, she screams her fury. In her hand is her spindle, its deadly thread unspooling as she moves. With the speed of a whip, it wraps itself around the gytrash, binding it to the grave as a spider binds a fly. The gytrash howls and struggles. Its powerful limbs are entangled

in the thread; it cannot escape. The sides of the grave begin to cave in upon it. The pile of earth it has dug out slides and topples down, drowning its howls and burying it completely. The ground shakes for a while as the gytrash fights its fate. At last, all is still.

The people of Goathland breathe again and come out of their hiding places. Gytha stands on the new grave. She looks back once towards her former friends and neighbours, and then, throwing her spindle far out over the moor she slowly rises into the air and disappears into the night.

The villagers never see either of them again.

# 5

# Hobs
# and Such

## On Hobs

*Western Moors*

A list of all the hobs (or hobmen, or hobthrushes, as they are sometimes called) that live in Yorkshire would be a long one. Mulgrave Wood, Runswick Bay, Castleton, Obthrush Roque (Hobthrush Rock!) all had a hob and Pickering was positively infested with them; there was the Leaholme Hob, Hob o'Hasly Bank, t'Hob o' Brakken Howe, the Scugdale Hob and no doubt many more just called t'Hob.

But what are hobs? The study of hob-lore is esoteric and yet curiously satisfying as they are cheery little creatures with little malice in them – except, like us, when unappreciated. They are related to hobbits – though they tend to dismiss these as 'Nowt but posh southerners'. They are small, brown, active and, usually, naked (in the Yorkshire climate this implies a considerable degree of toughness).

Like all hob-folk they are hole dwellers, though a few (like the Runswick Bay hob) live in caves. However, whatever hole they live in, they nearly all work in nearby farms, for they enjoy being useful and like the company of humans, with whom they have a pleasantly symbiotic relationship. Hobs excel in farm and domestic work, requiring human payment in the form of a dish of cream or some other food. Money means nothing to them, although they often make the farmer for whom they work rich. Though they themselves are seldom seen and many jobs are done, seemingly at night, any farm where they live is a lucky one where everything always goes well.

It appears that hobs are immortal; though there have not been any reliable studies on this, possibly because they outlive those who study them. They are a sub-branch of the Fair Folk by whom they are regarded as very primitive, principally because of their naked-ness ('So Palaeolithic!'). A hob's greatest ambition is to acquire clothes, lovely colourful clothes. Only when he – and hobs all seem to be 'he' unless, like dwarves, the sexes are indistinguishable, which seems unlikely when one considers their nakedness – only when he has got such clothes will he be regarded as having made it to the big time. Then he will no longer have to hear the scornful fairy cry of 'Here comes the grubby old hob with never a stitch to cover his ****'. He will instead become a hob aristocrat and never have to work again but spend eternity propping up the bar in fairy hills or footing it featly at fairy balls with his mates.

It was this desire to acquire bright clothes that, far back in the mists of antiquity, must have inspired the first hob to venture on a relation-ship with humans. No doubt there were hobs working on Greek and Roman farms, hoping perhaps, to gain a tiny chiton or embroidered tunic. As both nations made slaves do all their work it would have been slaves who benefitted most from hob assistance. No doubt it was they who began to make offerings of food to these useful little household gods. The desired clothes, however, were not so quickly forthcoming and so other strategies had to be developed over the centuries.

Humans are pretty stupid, according to hobs, but if you wait long enough they will eventually get the message. Hobs themselves are extremely patient and quite willing to wait hundreds of years for a result. One of them told me that the secret of success is for the hob to wait until there is a particularly sympathetic human, often a child, living on the farm and then to show himself 'accidentally on purpose'. The person is so shocked at the wretched nakedness of the hob that he or she goes away and makes some clothes for him. When the hob finds them the next night, he pulls them on with a merry whoop and disappears never to be seen (by the donor) again. I pointed out that the kind giver was rather badly repaid for his or her kindness, but I was told, hey, they had got all that work for centuries for the price of an evening bowl of cream, so what was their problem?

Very occasionally, the human gift of clothes will fail to meet hob standards. They are particularly insulted if given tiny copies of peasant smocks made of hemp. That will lose you your hob very quickly. At Sturfitt Hall near Reeth and Close House in Skipton-in-Craven the hobs left in a huff to find less class-ridden employment, crying:

> Gin hob mun ha'e nowt but a hardin hamp
> (If a hob has no more than a hempen smock)
> He'll come nae more to berry or stamp!
> He'll come no more to mow or thresh

The day of the hob seems, alas, to be almost over. The advent of machinery on farms has rendered most hobs jobless. Has it put an end to their hope of ever getting clothes? Although they have always been country dwellers, it seems possible that they, like foxes, will have no choice but to move into towns. I can foresee the day when some harassed cleaner will arrive early at the office block she (or he) cleans to find the hoovering done, the computer keys dusted, and the sinks and urinals in the lavatories polished. Let us hope that he (or she) will feel grateful enough to leave a suitable present for the unseen helper, for hobs are sensitive to slights of that sort and have been known to punish the ungrateful – as can be seen in the following tale …

## The Farndale Hob

Jonathan Gray was a wealthy farmer who lived in Farndale, near Kirby Moorside. His grandfather had had the good fortune to gain the friendship – and free labour – of a hob. This grandfather had been farming for many years before making the hob's acquaintance and had a particularly fine farm servant called Ralph who could shear or thresh or mow better than anyone else in the area.

One cold winter's day Ralph was caught in a sudden blizzard and frozen to death as he crossed the moor. Everyone in the dale was very sad and said that the farmer had lost the best thing on his farm.

Not long after Ralph's funeral, the farmer was awoken in the middle of the night by a thumping noise that seemed to come from the barn. He jumped out of bed wondering what on earth it could be; downstairs he met some of his servants who had also been woken by the noise.

'What do you think it is? Is it ghosts?' whispered one of the young farm lads who slept in an attic over the kitchen.

'Don't be daft, lad,' said the farmer, but he was worried. 'It sounds like someone's threshing!' They all listened in terrified silence. Soon the unmistakeable crack of a wooden flail on the stone floor of the barn was clearly recognised by everyone.

'But who'd thresh at night?' quavered the farmer's wife, gripping his arm. 'Oh my goodness, perhaps it's our Ralph come back from the dead?'

The farmer saw panic spreading. 'Nonsense,' he said firmly, 'there's no such thing as ghosts. Get off to bed, everyone, it'll be one of the hands trying to get into my good books. Get to bed, I say!'

In the morning he and his wife, who would not let him go alone, went down early to the barn. Something had certainly happened to the wheat stored there. The pile of sheaves heaped at one end of the barn had halved, while at the other end there were two new piles, one of shining brown wheat grains and the other, much larger, of all the husks and straw that had been threshed off, waiting to be turned into chaff for animal feed.

'That's never a right man's work,' gasped the farmer's wife. 'It'd tek ten men to do that much in a night. Even our Ralph couldn't have done it!' The farmer ran his fingers through the wheat and rubbed a few grains between his palms.

'Wheat seems right enough, though.'

'Do you think it's Ralph's ghost?'

'Nay lass, Ralph's in Heaven like the Good Book says – dinna you mind the parson? This is summat else. I reckon we've got us a hob!'

And so it proved. The hob continued to work. Come hay-time he mowed half a field a night and carted it home too; at shearing he sheared as many sheep in one night as three farmhands could do in two days. At harvest he reaped and loaded a whole wagon by himself. The other farm labourers might have complained at losing paid work, but as the farmer could now afford to rent more land to expand the farm, they were all still employed. The whole place flourished.

The farmer was a wise man and knew better than to kill the goose that laid the golden egg.

'The labourer is worthy of his hire!' he said to his wife, so every evening she put out a big jug of cream for the hob, and every morning she found it empty (and washed and neatly turned upside-down on the draining board).

Well, years went by and the hob went on working. The farm remained prosperous, the garden flourished and the workers always seemed lucky and cheerful. When the old man died, he passed the farm on to his son who continued to value the hob and never forgot his jug of cream. When the time came, he, in his turn, passed the farm on to his son Jonathan and his wife Margery. In his will, he reminded them never to forget to whom they owed the farm's prosperity.

Unfortunately, after a few years Margery fell ill and died when the children were still quite small. As was the custom in those days, Jonathan soon married again in order to provide his children with someone to look after them. The new wife seemed a pleasant enough woman, never unkind to the children, but she had come from a hill farm where strict economy was essential for survival. She was used to keeping a tight hand on the purse strings. When Jonathan told her about the hob's cream she could hardly believe her ears. A whole jug of cream that might have been made into butter, wasted! She did not want to offend her new husband so she grudgingly put out the cream every night, but it pained her careful mind sorely.

One evening it was too much for her. At the market that day she had seen how expensive butter had become and that she could have made a handsome profit if only she had had more of it to sell. That night she put out a jug of whey (the thin watery stuff left over from butter making, normally given to the pigs).

The very next day all luck left the place; the tireless hob stopped working. There was no more help with the shearing or mowing or threshing. Worse still, lots of things that had gone well before began to go badly. The hob who had worked so hard for the farm's prosperity now began to work for its destruction. The butter would not come, no matter how long the dairymaids churned; the wife's nicely fattened hens were carried off by a fox; the mould on the cheese was a thick blue fur so that no one would buy it; the ale brewed and the bread baked were all spoiled by some strange unpleasant yeast.

Now you might think that if the farmer's wife had started to put out the cream again the hob might have come around. But not she! On the contrary, she was so angry and upset at what was happening that she swore by the Bible that the hob would never have another mouthful of cream from her.

'He's nobbut an evil boggart!' she declared to her alarmed husband. 'Don't you try to change my mind. I've sworn on the Bible!'

No one likes being called a boggart.

'I'll boggart them!' thought the hob and he began to act like one.

Soon the house was almost unbearable to live in. No one could sleep for the banging of kettles, the clashing of pewter plates, the crashing of pottery and the clanging of fire irons. The house echoed every night with groans, howls, rude noises, thumps, rattles. People were tripped up; beds were lifted and then dropped with a bone-shaking crash; candles were blown out; people were pinched black and blue. It was not long before no farmhand would stay anywhere near the farmhouse.

Jonathan and his wife endured this for a few months, but the farm was going to pieces; they were both at the end of their tether. Nearly all the money made by Jonathan's father and grandfather had gone. They were forced to give up the tenancy their family had held for so many generations and take another on a much smaller farm.

'It will be harder work for us, but at least we'll be free of that hob!' said Jonathan.

The family packed up, with many tears from the children, very unhappy about leaving their home. The old carthorse was put between the shafts of their last remaining cart, which was piled high with all the furniture that remained after the family had paid off its immediate creditors.

They still owed the landlord part of the year's rent, but there was no way they could pay it so they left the farm late one night, doing a 'moonlight flit' to avoid being seen by the landlord's bailiff.

Jonathan looked back at the place where his family had been so happy.

'Enjoy yourself!' he shouted to the hob. 'Make someone else's life a misery, why don't you!' Then he turned away and shook the reins.

At the bend in the road, they met one of Jonathan's neighbours who had been out late with his dog, shooting rabbits.

'Hey Jonathan!' he said. 'What are you all doing at this time of night?'

Before Jonathan could reply, from the top of the furniture piled on the back of the cart, came a strange gravelly voice:

'We're flittin'!' it said, gleefully.

## On Fairies

One day, when I was about twelve, one of my pencils began to walk across the floor. I did not believe it at first. I got out of bed and went over to it. It was definitely my pencil – I could even see the toothmarks on it where I had chewed the end, 'Wow!' I thought, 'So magic really does exist!'

I bent down to get a better look; a little frightened but wondering what it would do next. Then, as though someone had flicked a switch the vision of the pencil disappeared and was replaced with that of a large, crawling hawkmoth caterpillar (I had been raising them). It was not just a matter of my imagining the pencil: my eyes had actually seen it. Brains interpret the information the eyes send them as best they can, according to what the owner knows about and what is expected.

In the twilight, when shadows deceive our eyes, or in the dark when all our ancient senses are particularly alert, we may literally see strange things. If we expect to see fairies, then fairies we will see; if extraterrestrials or demons or angels or just moving leaves, then we will see them instead; it all depends on a confusing visual situation and the expectations of the viewer.

Belief in fairies was waning by the time the genial vicars, who collected so many folk stories, walked the hills of Yorkshire. To admit to such a belief had become a badge of foolishness. That does not mean that it had not been widespread not so long before, or that it had actually died out. Fairies are jealous things and speaking of them has always been considered bad luck, especially where roads are dark and lonely; life was uncertain enough without fairy enmity. The tales of fairies we have are only the tales that ordinary people were prepared to tell someone 'educated' – there must have been many more!

## THE FAIRIES OF ELBOLTON HILL

### Nidderdale

'Thoo's niver going by Elbolton Hill? Well, watch out for fairies!' Frank's friend gave him a parting slap on the back and waved a cheery goodbye.

'I's not afeart. Never worry about me!' Frank headed off into the spring night. It was ideal for walking; the moon shone as brightly as day; the scents of hawthorn and elder rose strongly in the still cool air. It was pure pleasure to be out in it.

As he walked, Frank hummed 'Barbry Allen', a tune popular in his village, but finding it too slow and sad to walk to, he switched and sang 'The Bold Dragoon' and was soon stepping out in fine style, no longer humming but singing with gusto. He loved singing and thought himself rather talented.

The dragoon with his broaden sword
He made their bones to rattle …

Before him the distinctive shape of Elbolton Hill rose up strange in the moonlight. Frank felt a little flutter of fear mixed with excitement. He remembered as a lad going down into Navvy Noodle Hole on the side of the hill, a place where everyone knew the fairies lived. He had done it as a dare and nearly been frightened out of his wits, but the fairies had not been in that day, and he climbed back out of the hole with nothing worse than a few grazes and a bumped head.

Some of his friends kept treasured elf bolts they had picked up near the hill, little leaf-shaped pieces of worked flint like arrowheads that fairies shot at cattle or people who annoyed them. If they hit you, you got sick; everyone knew that.

Frank's granny had told him a lot about fairies, and despite all the dangers, he wanted to see them very much. He did not think that they were as evil as they were painted; after all, they liked music, dancing and merriment, so they were not so very different to him.

As he reached the footpath along the side of Elbolton Hill he stopped singing and walked along as quietly as possible. Who knew? Tonight might be the night he got his wish.

The bushes on the hill were very black, but a little way along he thought he could see a light that came from a source other than the moon. He stopped and listened hard. Yes! A silvery tinkle of music, a faint wash of laughter. He was in luck! Delighted excitement flowed through him. Slowly and carefully he approached the light, creeping along behind the tall drystone walls that bordered the path.

The fairies were holding a party in the centre of a big fairy toadstool ring (Frank was pleased to see that his granny had been right about that). There were little trestle tables set up, spread with many sorts of food and drink where fairies were enjoying themselves. Nearby there was a group of tiny fiddlers sawing away madly on tiny fiddles. They were playing such jolly reels and jigs that Frank's feet started tapping almost by themselves. Some fairies were dancing to the music on their own, their little feet a blur as they leapt and twirled. There were a few couples, exquisitely graceful, swinging each other around as lightly as a sycamore key spins to the ground.

Frank settled down to watch, noting everything to tell his friends and family about later.

'Wouldn't the bairns just love it!' he thought.

The fairies were all dressed in different shades of green, from the almost-black of cedar, through emerald and pea green to the palest eau de Nil. Their wings were transparent like those of a dragonfly, though not as stiff, flapping rather than buzzing.

Now the dances were changing; the fairies were joining together into rings and swirling in and out in complicated figures, rising

into the air, swooping down, intertwining but never hitting each other, like gnats over a pool.

Frank watched open-mouthed, hardly able to distinguish the individual figures of the dances, though he was a good dancer himself. After a while, the company ceased leaping and went for more refreshments, though they showed no obvious signs of fatigue. They ate from silver plates and drank from golden goblets while a master of ceremonies spoke at length in a high little voice. He was apparently introducing the next event for soon a fairy woman came forwards and began to sing beautifully. Frank tried to remember the tune, though he could not understand the words. Afterwards a harper played music so haunting that tears trickled down Frank's cheeks.

And so the entertainment went on; one after another of the fairies taking his or her turn. It reminded Frank of the sort of good evening he and his friends sometimes had at the pub – though rather more elegant, of course. Thinking about this he was suddenly filled with the desire to sing.

'Happen they'll like 'The Bonny Bunch of Roses'!' he thought, standing up. 'Na' then. Ah'll sing a song if tha loikes!' he cried to the little master of ceremonies.

Instantly he realised that he had made a mistake. The fairies began to buzz like a disturbed beehive. Then they rushed hither and thither in confusion, and, seeing Frank, they all rose up and flew at him, biting, kicking, pinching and throwing small stones as hard as they could.

Frank was a big tough Yorkshireman, used to the vicious biting cleggs and clouds of midges on the moors, so he was not much damaged, but he was dismayed at breaking up the party and worried that he would hurt the fairies as he tried gently to bat them away from his face. Almost by accident, his big hand closed over a particularly persistent one. It was too good an opportunity to miss; he thrust the struggling creature hastily into his pocket.

'It'll be summat to show to t'bairns!' he thought guiltily as, in a few long strides, he crossed the fairy ring and reached the path again.

The fairies followed him for a while, presumably shouting insults and threats after him, for he could hear their tinkling voices all the way down the hill.

He reached home with great excitement. Who else had ever caught a fairy? He imagined displaying it to everyone – maybe even showing it at the fair! He could see the sign now: 'Never Previously brought before the Public! Frank Metcalf and his Amazing Flying Friend!' See the Queen (or the King if the fairy should turn out to be male) of the Fairies Dance!

He'd have a little crown made!

His children were all asleep in bed but he insisted on them being woken up. Then he held them still yawning but spellbound with an account of his adventures on Elbolton Hill.

'And now!' he said, wishing that he could conjure up a drum roll. 'I've got summat that'll amaze you all … It's a real fairy what I caught tonight!' He put his hand into his pocket, but when he drew it out … there was nothing there!

# 6

# MYSTERIES

## FOUNDING STORIES

Imagine a world with no safety nets: no pensions, no benefits, no NHS. To be poor in that world is to always walk a tightrope. As long as you can work, you can eat. If you cannot work, you instantly become reliant on the kindness of others to keep you alive. You can beg, or steal, or borrow from you neighbours, but you have become a dropped stitch in the fabric of your community.

This is why monasteries, whose duty it was to provide food and medical care for the poor, were so important in the Middle Ages: they were the only reasonably reliable source of help apart from your neighbours or family members who were often as poor as yourself.

The north of England was impoverished compared with the fertile south where rich landowners could afford to give more charity. In the harsh conditions of much of North Yorkshire, famine was a familiar visitor, but northern lords by tradition had to put much of their money into weapons and soldiers in order to combat Scottish raids, which often came as far south as York. Henry VIII's destruction of the monasteries was felt much harder here than further south.

It is hard to know how well Christianity was understood by illiterate Yorkshire peasants at the time, but its simpler tenets, at any rate, provided an essential mental security against the evils of the world. The image of the monastery represented continuity and stability in the brief hard life of a peasant. The magic words of the priest, the magic substance of the Mass, the magic holy water that could heal the sick were the poor's own strong weapons against the enemy that stalked behind their left shoulder, waiting to pounce.

Whatever criticisms people might have had of individual degenerate monks, love and respect for monasteries as institutions was widespread. Stories illustrating the holiness of the local monastery were important for local prestige and it was natural to enhance their glory by ascribing supernatural aid to their original founding. Two of such stories follow.

## The White Birds

### Hambledon Hills

Once there were some monks at Byland Abbey, who set out to find a place to build another monastery. They were Cistercians, vowed to live in the inhospitable and barren parts of the earth. With nothing but a strong faith that God would show them the perfect place to plant their new home, they wandered many many miles. They remembered how faithful monks had carried St Cuthbert's body for years until they were shown the right place to bury him. There they had built an abbey and now Durham with its great hilltop cathedral was famous.

When night came the Byland monks slept, wrapped in their robes, in the thorny shelter of some whin bushes high on a lonely hillside.

That night their leader and future abbot had a dream. He saw a woman walking towards him leading a little boy by the hand. The woman was astonishingly beautiful and it worried the monk that she was alone in such a desolate place.

'Lady,' he said, 'what are you doing alone here in this barren spot with such a young child?'

She smiled and said, 'I am often to be found in deserted places. I have come from Rievaulx to Byland and now I am going to a new monastery.'

The abbot-to-be felt a lifting of his spirit. 'Lady, we too are of Byland and are seeking a place to found a new holy house, but we do not know this land and are wandering like blind men. Of your courtesy show us the way to this new monastery you speak of.'

'You were once of Byland,' she replied, gravely, 'but now you are of Jervaulx.' She turned to the little boy and asked him to be the monks' guide. 'For I am called away …' and with that, she vanished.

Then in the dream – though it felt more real than any dream – the abbot rose up with his monks and prepared to follow the little boy who, before setting off, first pulled a branch from a nearby tree.

The monks walked behind him for what seemed like hours until at last in a beautiful green valley the boy stopped and thrust the branch into the ground. Straightaway it began to grow and as it did birds began to fly to it. At last it stood tall and fair and filled with little white birds who sang sweetly. The child turned to the monks. 'Here shall God be adored for a while!' he said and as he spoke he changed, filled with glory, becoming the radiant Christ child who blessed them all.

When the abbot awoke, he sprang up with joy and told the others his dream. He led them unerringly to the green valley he had seen in it and there, by the River Ure, they began to build their new monastery. They called it Jervaulx (meaning Ure valley).

In time Jervaulx Abbey became great and powerful. Surprisingly, it was famous for its horse breeding and its Wensleydale cheese as well as its piety. Its glory came to an end when Henry VIII closed it and hanged its last abbot for treason after the Pilgrimage of Grace. His name remains, beautifully engraved into the stone of his cell in the Tower of London: 'ADAM SEDBAR: ABBAS IOREVALL.' But the ruins of his abbey also remain, carpeted in flowers and still full of the singing of birds.

## THE LOAF OF BREAD

### Harrogate area

The River Skell flowed through a wilderness of rocks and trees. There had once been religious foundations in the valley, but Viking raids destroyed them all and the folk who had once lived there had fled long years before. It was in just such deserted places that the Benedictine monks of the twelfh century delighted to live, abandoning the troublesome world for a life of peace, abstinence and prayer.

Richard, the prior of St Mary's Abbey in York had tried hard to revitalise the religious spirit of his monastery. There was a feeling abroad at the time that monasteries, once the abode of truly holy men, were becoming increasingly degenerate. Richard's efforts were not successful enough to satisfy twelve of the most critical monks. Having got permission from the archbishop, they left the monastery to found a new monastery on the deserted banks of the Skell where they hoped to follow the rule of their founder, St Benedict, more strictly.

It was winter when the twelve monks arrived at the Skell. They were completely without any form of shelter and the only thing between them and the bitter east wind were seven yew trees. (It is said that two still stand.) They had some basic tools, so with great labour in the freezing wind and hampered by the short days they managed to build a simple hut against the bole of a great elm tree.

Food was scarce – less than scarce – for what food could they find in the barren winter fields beyond dry grass and elm bark? Somehow, they survived that first terrible winter and their very tenacity attracted others to join them. The next spring they laid out fields, moving many rocks and trees, and began the hard work of cultivating the earth. A small group of wooden monastic buildings began to rise, but the monks were still dirt poor and short of food. It is to be hoped that they did not regret their choice to leave York!

One day a traveller knocked at the door. When the porter opened it, he found a man weak with hunger collapsed outside. 'Food! For the love of Christ!' he begged.

The porter was in a dilemma, because he knew that there was practically no food in the place. 'I fear we have nothing to give you, my poor son,' he said.

'For our sweet Saviour's sake give me a loaf of bread or you will see me die here at your feet!'

In desperation, the porter went to the abbot and explained the situation. 'We have only two and a half loaves left and we need those for the carpenters and the other workers when they come back from work.'

'Well,' said the abbot, 'we can't begrudge a loaf of bread to a starving man! One and a half loaves will have to be sufficient for us lucky people who are not yet starving.'

The porter took one of the precious loaves to the traveller, who blessed the monks fervently as he at last began to fill his empty belly.

There were only a few mouthfuls of bread for each of the monks who had been working and nothing at all for those who had not, but filled with the happiness of having helped a stranger in trouble, they did not complain.

A few hours later, there was another knock on the door and the porter opened it to find two men with a large cart standing outside. From the cart came the intoxicating smell of fresh bread.

'Sir Porter,' said one of the men, 'the Lord of Knaresborough Castle, Sir Eustace Fitzhugh, hearing that you are short of food, has sent you this cartload of bread.'

The monks all rejoiced and praised God, believing that He had seen their plight.

It was from this time that Fountains Abbey, as it became known, began to flourish until at last its fame spread throughout the region and it became rich and powerful. The twelve brave founders were always honoured, but whether those that followed in the years after them, as the abbey grew ever richer, were as holy or as ascetic is less certain.

## SEMER WATER

*Dales*

Raydale at the head of Wensleydale is a place of kelds (springs). Their wild waters, flowing from the mysterious limestone caverns that lie beneath Wither Fell, Addlebrough and Stalling Busk, break out into many little becks and flow into Semer Water, one of the few lakes in the Dales. There are waterfalls too, sparkling in the sunlight, white in the rain showers that rush up the valley. It is a hard place in winter, though, when the roads are icy and the tracks over the hill are as treacherous as the peat bogs they skirt.

On one such winter's day, an old beggar was slowly making his way towards the entrance of the prosperous town that lay in Raydale valley. Where he had come from, why he was travelling, even what his name was, is not told in the story. Perhaps he himself had forgotten these things in a hard life. Or perhaps he was not what he seemed …

He stopped before the first small cottage he came to and approached the door. Before he had even raised his hand to knock, however, it was opened by a woman holding a broom in her hand. 'What do you want?' she asked suspiciously, taking in his way-worn clothes and rag-covered feet.

'A drink of water, missus?' the beggar asked humbly.

'What's wrong with beck water?' she demanded. 'Get along with you!' She slammed the door before the beggar had time to tell her that the becks were all frozen over.

Slowly he moved on up the main street.

The next cottage he stopped at had a fine first storey that over-hung the street. A tailor was sitting cross-legged on a table in the big sunlit window of the upstairs parlour. The old man looked up and the tailor looked down. Then the tailor leant forwards and opened the window.

'I've nowt for beggars,' he shouted. 'Go away and stop cluttering up my street!'

'A little water, maister? A crust of bread?'

'Mary!' shouted the tailor angrily. 'Water for the beggar!'

A little dormer window opened above him and a grinning maid emptied a chamber pot into the street, missing the old man by a whisker. The tailor laughed uproariously and slammed his window shut.

Shaking his head sadly, the old man continued up the street. Soon he came to a large house with fine carving on its timbers – a prosperous butcher's house. Surely, such a well-off man could spare something for a beggar.

The beggar knew better than to knock at the front door. He went around to the kitchen at the back. A smart lad opened the door and peered out.

'Can you spare awt to eat or drink, young sir?'

The lad threw his eyes up to heaven. 'What sort of gowk are you? Hasn't anyone told you? Maister can't bear your sort. Get going before he finds you here!'

And so it went all the way through the town. In one house the cook pretended that the old man must belong to a gang of thieves come to spy on the place; in another the man of the house, tankard in hand, lectured him on working hard instead of being a layabout. 'The undeserving poor are leeches sucking the wealth out of this country!' he said.

In yet another, where a fat family were about to begin an enormous dinner, he was told that charity begins at home. 'If we gave to every beggar who knocks on the door we'd be as poor as pauper soup.'

It seemed that the whole town had forgotten what it was to be poor and old and cold and desperate.

At the top of the village he was directed to the priest's house by the warmly dressed inn-keeper's wife.

'It's the Church should care for ancients like you. The priest is a man of God, after all, or so he tells us as he pockets our tithes!'

Limping badly by now the beggar followed the directions and soon came to a handsome stone house surrounded by a high wall. He pushed open the gate and made his way to the back door. As he passed the dining room window, he saw the priest sitting at a table laden with food. There was fish and venison, pies, a great sirloin of beef.

The priest graciously left his meal for a moment to talk to the old man. He kindly informed him that he was very sorry, but that there was nothing suitable in the house to give a beggar. He would, however, say a prayer for him that very night and God would provide for him sooner or later if he only had faith. Then, with the air of someone who had done a noble deed, he smiled, nodded sympathetically and closed the door firmly.

The old man shambled back along the garden path. There was only one more place to try: the castle. There it stood, rich and powerful. The main gates were open, for this was a time of peace. There were a few soldiers lolling around in the courtyard eating bread, cheese and apples. When they saw the old man, they began to make fun of him.

'Where are you gannin' Granddad?' they shouted. They stood over him and barred his way until he told them what his business was. 'Oh food, eh? Well they've just fed t' swine. Would thy lordship would care to join thy friends?' They pushed him around from one to another, but as he did not protest, they got bored after a while and let him go, throwing their apple cores at his back as he limped towards the kitchen.

There his reception was even worse. The young scullions, black with soot and greasy from scouring pots, chased him around the room, hallooing and waving ladles and knives. Then they grabbed him by his skinny arms and threatened to put him on the spit next to the fat boar that was browning nicely there. In the end, the cook heard the noise and came in to the kitchen in a rage. He beat the boys into some sort of order, but he threw the old beggar out and told him that if he caught him doddering about there again he would set the dogs on him. The beggar could hear the dogs howling, mercifully shut up in their kennels.

Even more dishevelled now the beggar ran the gauntlet of the soldiers again and patiently walked back over the castle bridge. There he saw a brave sight coming down the road. The baron who owned the castle was returning from some outing. He was surrounded by his servants in bright livery. The beggar stepped forward into the path of his horse and knelt. Surely knight's honour would not allow him to leave an old man without shelter.

'My lord! My lord!' he cried. 'Help for God's sake!'

The baron's horse snorted but his master reined him in. 'What can you possibly want from me, old man?'

'Food, Sir, shelter for one in desperate need. I asked your folk but they taunted me and threw me out.'

'Get your insolent body out of my path!' roared the baron. 'Where are the dogs?'

The beggar cringed and shuffled hastily out of the way as the baron's horse sprang forwards over the bridge. Soon the castle's doors were fastened behind their lord.

The sun was setting now. The old man had nowhere to go except onwards. The road out of the town was steep and icy, but he trudged forward up out of the valley; it was filling with grey evening mist. On the brown winter hills the last sun-light still glowed, but the cold was already creeping out from the shadows.

At the last turn of the road before the moor brow there was a cottage. It did not look very inviting for it was a single-storeyed low building, thatched with turf, not much different to a cow byre. Still, the old man had caught a glimpse of cheerful firelight shining from the single window, so he knocked tentatively.

The door was opened by a wiry middle-aged man with a weather-beaten face.

'I'm sorry to trouble you –' began the old man, but the shepherd (for that is what he was) gestured for him to enter even before he finished his sentence.

'Come in, grandfeyther,' he said, 'come in and get a warm by the fire. You look half-starved with cold!' Gratefully the old man entered and stretched out his old trembling hands to the warmth.

'Sit down. There's nobbut one chair but I can tek t'stool.' The shepherd indicated a roughly carved armchair and the old man sank gratefully into it.

'Thank you, maister, I've been walking all day.'

The shepherd looked thoughtful. 'Thoo'll not have etten, then, I guess. Not if thoo've been down yonder. They're so near down there they'd skin a flea if they could catch it. Dinna thoo worry,

I've bread an' cheese an' a slip of fatty bacon'll set tha up like a lord. A drop of ale too, if thoo wants.'

'But that's your meal.'

'Eh well, they say shared bread is sweeter! Put thy feet up while I fettle it.'

And so the old man got food and drink, little enough, it is true, but given with as much cheerful insistence as if the shepherd had a full storeroom. They chatted together after the meal, with the old man telling of his travels, the shepherd of the strange ways of mountain sheep. Then the shepherd made up a bed for himself by the fire, insisting that the old man sleep on his rough pallet, covered with warm sheepskins.

When the shepherd woke the next morning the old man was not there.

'He's left betimes,' he thought, sorry to lose the chance of further talk, for his was a lonely life. As was his custom he opened the door and stepped out to see what the weather was doing. Then he saw that his guest had not gone. He was standing with his back to the cottage, staring down at the still-sleeping town. It seemed to the shepherd that he looked taller and straighter than he had been the night before and that the light of the newly risen sun had changed his white hair to gold.

'I hope tha slept sound?' he asked. At the sound of the shepherd's voice, the old man turned towards him. The shepherd gasped, doubting his own eyes. Where were the lines, the wrinkles? Where were the rags? The person who stood there dressed in shining robes was young and beautiful – beautiful in a way that made the shepherd tremble with fear.

'Wha is thoo, (who are you) my lord?' he whispered, falling to his knees.

'Do not be afraid!' said the young man. 'You merit nothing but the highest praise. You took in a stranger and fed him when you had almost nothing. May you be happy! It is those without kindness who should tremble!' He stared once more at the town and there was no mercy in his gaze. The sun began to dim as he grew taller and more terrible. Black clouds appeared from nowhere, borne on a rising wind. He flung out his hands in a wide gesture that seemed to embrace the whole town. Then he cried in a loud voice:

'I call thee Semerwater, rise fast, rise deep, rise free!

Whelm all except the little house that fed and sheltered me!'

Instantly the black clouds over the town exploded with thunder and lightning; rain poured down. From every keld and beck in the valley great gouts of water spouted up in torrents, foaming and rushing with waterfalls becoming geysers. Spray filled the valley. The roar of water grew and grew; it was deafening but not

so deafening that the shepherd could not hear the screams of the townsfolk as they tried in vain to escape their doom.

The radiant figure turned once more to the shepherd who was still kneeling, filled with fear and grief. There was a brief smile and a hand raised in blessing, then without another word the angel spread its magnificent wings and flew away into the pale-blue sky that still shone beyond the rolling clouds.

The rain fell all day. Then the clouds vanished and the shepherd, daring once more to look into the valley, saw no town at all, but only the low winter sun shining on the calm grey water of a lake.

## The Devil's Bridge

*Nidderdale*

Do not call it that! To name the Devil is to call him up, they say. Call it Dibble's Bridge; that would be safer – and yet its evil builder, for once, claimed no deadly price for building it as he did in other places.

Take Kilgram Bridge, for example, that straddles the Ure between Thornton Steward at the lower end of Wensleydale and Jervaux Abbey. In the past, the villagers' efforts to build a bridge strong enough to cope with the force of the river in flood kept failing. Wooden bridge after wooden bridge was washed away, leaving them and their animals stranded. In desperation, they turned to someone well known for his ability to build in difficult places: the Devil! There is hardly a dangerous valley in Britain that is not spanned by a bridge attributed to him. But he demanded a high fee: the life of the first being to cross. The Thornton Steward villagers were desperate; they agreed to his terms and the very next day they woke to find a splendid new bridge over the Ure. Everyone rejoiced. All that remained was to find a way to cheat the Devil of a human victim.

Attempts to get hens or sheep to cross ended in failure. Cats sat and washed themselves; dogs crept away with their tails between their legs. The villagers stared at their brand-new bridge in dismay. Would they ever be able to use it?

Then a hard-hearted local shepherd had an idea. He made his sheepdog, Grim, sit and wait at the entrance to the bridge. Then he swam over the river, climbed out and called to Grim from the other side. The faithful dog ran towards him but the moment he touched the further shore he fell dead. The bridge was thereafter called – if you will believe it – Kill Grim Bridge (now known as Kilgram).

A similar bargain made with the Devil is told about many bridges, but Dibbles Bridge is different. It was built because of a generous man and a tasty lunch.

The little village of Thorpe-sub-Montem (Thorpe Underhill) was once famous throughout the Dales for its cobblers. Odd though it might seem that such an out-of-the-way place should have so many, there were enough monasteries and abbeys in the area to make it worthwhile training up sons in the craft.

One of the best was Ralph Calvert, who made and mended the shoes and sandals of the monks of Fountains Abbey. It was said that he could make three pairs of shoes in the time it took another man to make two. He also made harnesses, belts and the delicate leather hoods worn by hawks.

Twice a year, at Christmas and Midsummer, he would load up a big wicker pack with all the commissions he had been given six months before, plus any new things he had thought of, and set off on the thirty-mile trip to the monastery. By Burnsall he went, and Langerton Hill, to Pateley Bridge and then on to Fountains.

His way took him sometimes on moor, sometimes on the high road, but there was one place he dreaded going through. It was where he had to cross the River Dibb at the dark bottom of a steep hill. There was a ford but he never knew whether it would be easy to cross or difficult, because the river could rise very swiftly.

He did not hurry. Sometimes he would break his journey halfway, sleeping out in the fields in the summer, or staying in a little wayside inn in the winter. The following day he would arrive at the abbey where he was always welcomed warmly and well looked after in the monastery's guesthouse. The monks were good to him; they never haggled more than was polite over the prices he charged them and always paid him properly. Best of all, they liked a bit of a gossip quite as much as he did. Altogether it was a good way of life and he enjoyed it.

One summer's day, having spent a pleasant evening at the abbey, he set off for home with a new load of shoes and sandals to mend. He was feeling happy, for the day was sunny but not too hot for walking, and, even better, he had a bag of food for the journey, put together by one of the monastery's many cooks. The moors above Pateley were looking very fine that day, the heather on the verge of coming into flower and the gorse smelling sweetly after the heavy rains that had fallen during the night.

As Ralph descended towards the River Dibb, however, he became aware of the sound of roaring, and as he came down to the ford, he saw swirling water laced with foam. He realised that he would not be able to cross that day. He scratched his head. He could either wait until the water went down, which could take hours, or he could walk along the bank to Appletreewick and then double back to Thorpe – a long way. Neither option appealed to him but, being a cheerful soul who took problems in his stride, he sat down on a rock in the sun and began to unpack his lunch bag.

The monks had done him proud, with bread, meat, cheese, a small pie, boiled eggs, an onion or two, three apples and a small leather bottle of wine. As he unpacked, he began to sing to keep himself company (for people sang all the time in those days and didn't give a fig who heard them):

Sing luck-a-down, heigh down,
Ho down derry

To his surprise there came an answer!

Tol lol de rol, darel dol, dol de derry!

Ralph had been sure there was no one around, but when he looked up he saw, standing on the riverbank, gazing at its foaming water, a tall, black-haired, well-dressed stranger. Ralph continued the song to the end, singing alternate lines with the stranger, who turned and smiled at him. When the song was ended, Ralph jumped up and went over to greet him properly. They commiserated with each other on the state of the ford.

'I'm due in Grassington,' said the stranger. 'How about you?'

'I've me wife and bairns waiting for me in Thorpe,' said Ralph. They chatted about the weather and the state of the roads and then Ralph, taken with the stranger's friendly and engaging manner, invited him to share his meal.

The stranger seemed a little taken aback, but 'I don't mind if I do. It's more than kind of you!' he said.

They shared Ralph's sunlit rock and Ralph divided the monks' food between them. The stranger seemed quite touched, especially when the bottle of wine was passed to him.

'This wine is good!' he exclaimed. 'I don't know when I've tasted better – and believe me, I've emptied a few bottles!'

'It's from Fountains Abbey.'

'Ah yes. Those monks love their wine. I shall certainly remember to visit them!'

They ate and drank in companionable silence until at last the stranger said, 'You've been right kind to me, Ralph, so I feel that I owe it to you to reveal that I am actually Old Nick.'

Ralph was a bit surprised, but he was not one to fluster easily. 'Thoo's niver!' was all he replied, passing the bottle. Then he added, 'Well, what I say is, Old Nick's a gentleman and I'll niver hear nowt agin him again.'

The Devil wiped away a boiling tear with a spotless linen handkerchief. 'You're a good fellow. Might I have a bit more pie?'

'Help thaself,' said Ralph but he was thinking what a wonderful tale this would make. Him, Ralph Calvert, supping – well, picnicking – with the Devil!

'Only thing is,' he said, thinking out loud, 'who'll believe me?'

'Believe that I'm the Devil? I've just told you I am!'

'Yes, but how do I know that thoo's tellin' truth? Thoo'll have to prove it, thoo knows.'

The Devil was slightly miffed. 'No problem!'

'Go on then!'

'What do you want me to do?'

Ralph knew that he was pushing his luck, but he was not easily daunted. He looked around for an idea and his eye fell on the river.

'Gi'us a bridge here!'

The Devil considered. 'I could I suppose,' he said. 'Hmm, well, I like you and you've been very generous to me – a rare thing. All right, you're on. In four days' time, there'll be a bridge here. You can bring your little friends to see it. I'll waive my usual fee, too.'

'What were that then?'

'Mind your own business.'

'And do I get to keep ma soul?'

The Devil looked offended. 'Would I take your soul after we've broken bread together? Certainly not! What do you take me for?' He stood up and stretched. 'And so we must part.' He held his hand out tentatively. 'I don't suppose you'd shake hands with Old Nick, would you?'

Ralph held out his own hand. 'Reet willin'. Thoo's a grand ol' lad.' They solemnly shook hands, then the Devil took three steps and disappeared in a small puff of black smoke. Ralph packed up thoughtfully, swung his pack onto his back and trudged off along the river on the long detour to Appletreewick.

His wife would not believe the story, of course. Who would?

However, Ralph kept telling her that in four days the bridge would prove him right. 'It's a long walk theer!' she complained, but in the end her curiosity got the better of her. She told their neighbours the tale and they told their neighbours, and pretty soon there was no one in Thorpe who did not know about it. Naturally their curiosity also got the better of them and so by the fourth day it was a large crowd that set out on the road to the ford of Dibb. The local priest insisted on going with them, very dubious about the whole thing.

As they came down the valley the small boys running ahead began to shout and point. Soon everyone could see it: a fine, high, white-stone bridge spanning the river above the ford. Everyone rushed towards it but before the priest could remind them about Kilgrim and the Devil's usual price, several people had crossed and re-crossed it with no ill effects. It seemed that the Devil, true to his word, wanted no payment.

The priest insisted that the local stonemason carve a cross on each end of the bridge, just in case, and then everyone went home, well pleased with Ralph.

The next Christmas when Ralph was making his way, dry-shod and safe, over the swollen winter river, he paused in the middle of the new bridge and thought about his summer meal with Old Nick.

'Thoo's a Devil o' thy word,' he said, 'God bless!'

# 7

# WITCHES

## ON WITCHES

Now it may be that several thousand years ago, the witches of Yorkshire worshipped the Horned God or the White Goddess and danced naked in a frenzy of creative joy, but all that had ceased by the time their descendents were frightening folk in North Yorkshire in the eighteenth and nineteenth centuries. It was then that nearly all of the considerable number of North Yorkshire witch stories were collected. Sympathetic listeners like Richard Blakeborough heard first hand from grannies and grandfathers about the well-remembered old women of their youth who had cast spells on their cousins, cattle, bairns and so on. Their accounts of witch-strikes tell of real people who, for one reason or another had been labelled a witch.

It seems that the easiest way of acquiring such a reputation was to look suitably ugly and walk past people. Story after story relies on the bewitched just 'feeling that summat was not right' or that 'summat overcome me!' as they met a suitable candidate. Often the presence of witchcraft was merely determined by popular opinion that something unnatural was happening. It is unpleasantly similar to African tales of being bewitched by witch children.

However, witches there undoubtedly were; that is, people who believed themselves to have power, not just over the natural world but over the future as well. Some of these women were clearly genuinely nasty people who enjoyed the power given to them by their neighbours. Others acquired the more reputable title of wise women – a status always a little borderline. They were feared perhaps, but also consulted. There were wise men too, though no male witches: all the witches in these accounts appear to have been solitary females (though it is possible they once had families). There do not appear to have been any covens.

Fortunately, the cure for being witch-stricken was less draconian in Yorkshire than in other parts of the world – at least latterly when magistrates refused to prosecute for witchcraft. You first visited a chosen wise man or woman – the stories show that there were plenty to be had, all named and well known in their area – who would first determine if your problem was actually caused by a witch and then if so, which witch. He or she would then prescribe a counter spell. These mostly involved burning something horribly smelly, driving pins into bullock's hearts and perhaps sacrificing a black cat or cock. Bits of cloth torn from the clothes of a hanged man might also feature, and wickenwood (rowan) was essential. Quotations from the Bible or folk spells might be chanted. It seems the witch normally got off with nothing worse than a bit of unpleasantness as her spell backfired on her. In only one story is a witch ducked and that just seems to have been added for extra excitement. It may be that the women who actually held themselves out as witches were a secret social resource, consulted about sexual matters, love potions, getting revenge or pregnant, and so on.

## The Wise Woman of Littondale

### Wharfedale

In the year 17— a solitary cottage stood in a lonely gill not far from Arncliffe. A more wretched habitation the imagination cannot picture, it contained a single room inhabited by an old woman called Bertha, who was, throughout the valley, accounted a wise woman.

I was at that time very young and unmarried, and far from having any dread of her would frequently talk to her and was always glad when she called at my father's house. She was tall, thin and haggard. Her eyes were sunk deep in their sockets and her hoarse masculine voice was anything but pleasant. The reason I took such delight in her company was because she was possessed of great historical knowledge and related events that had occurred two or three centuries ago in such a detailed manner that many a time I believed that she had seen them for herself.

In the autumn of 17— I set out one evening to visit her cottage. I had never seen inside and was determined to. I knocked at the gate and she told me to come in. I entered. The old woman was seated on a three-legged stool by a peat fire, surrounded by three cats and an old sheepdog.

'Well,' she exclaimed. 'What brings you here?'

'Don't be offended,' I answered. 'I've never seen inside your cottage and wanted to do so. I also wished to see you perform some of your "incantations".' Bertha noticed that I spoke the last word ironically.

'So you doubt my power, think me an imposter and consider my incantations mere jugglery? Well, you may change your mind. Sit down and in less than half an hour you shall see evidence of my power greater than I have allowed anyone else to witness!'

I obeyed and approached the fireside, looking round the room as I did so. The only furnishings were three stools, an old deal table, a few pans, pictures of Merlin, Nostradamus and Michael Scott, a cauldron and a mysterious sack. The witch, having sat by me a few minutes, rose and said, 'Now for our incantation; watch me but don't interrupt.' She then drew a chalk circle on the floor and in the midst of it placed a chafing dish filled with burning embers; on this she fixed the cauldron that she had half-filled with water.

She then told me to stand on the opposite side of the circle. She opened the sack and taking from it various ingredients threw them into the pot. Amongst other things I noticed a skeleton head, bones of different sizes and the dried carcasses of some small animals. All the time she did this she continued muttering some words in an unknown language.

At length the water boiled and the witch, presenting me with a glass, told me to look through it at the cauldron. I did so and saw a figure enveloped in the steam. At the first glance I did not know what to make of it, but soon I recognised the face of N—, a good friend of mine. He was dressed in his usual way but seemed unwell and pale. I was astonished and trembled.

The figure having vanished, Bertha removed the cauldron and put out the fire.

'Now!' she said. 'Do you doubt my power? I have brought before you the form of a person who is some miles from here, I am no imposter!'

I only wanted to get out of there but as I was about to leave Bertha said, 'Stop! I haven't finished with you. I will show you something more wonderful. Tomorrow at midnight go and stand on Arncliffe Bridge and look at the water on the left side of it. Don't be afraid. Nothing will hurt you.'

'Why should I go? It's a lonely place. Can I take someone with me?'

'No!'

'Why not?'

'Because the charm will be broken,'

'What charm?'

'I'm not going to tell you any more. Do it. You will not be harmed.'

That night I lay awake unable to sleep and during the next day I was so preoccupied that I was unable to attend to any business.

Night came and I went to Arncliffe Bridge. I shall never forget the scene; it was a lovely night; the full moon was sailing peacefully through a clear deep-blue cloudless sky and its silver beams were dancing on the waters of the Skirfare beck. The stillness was broken only by the murmuring of the stream, while the scattered cottages and the autumn woods all united in a picture of calm and perfect beauty.

I leaned against the left battlement of the bridge, trying to be calm. I waited in fear for a quarter of an hour, half an hour, an hour. Nothing happened. I listened; all was silent. I looked around; I saw nothing. Surely, I thought, it must be midnight by now. Bertha has made a fool of me! I breathed more freely. Then I jumped as

the clock of the neighbouring church suddenly chimed. I had mistaken the hour. I resolved to stay a little longer.

Then, as I gazed in the stream, I heard a low moaning sound and saw the water violently troubled. The disturbance continued for a few moments before it ceased and the river became calm and peaceful again

I wondered what it could mean. Who moaned? What caused the disturbance? Full of fear I hurried home, but turning the corner of the lane that led to my father's house, I was startled as a huge dog crossed my path. A Newfoundland, I thought. It looked at me sadly. 'Poor fellow!' I exclaimed. 'Have you lost your master? Come home with me until we find him. Come on!' The dog followed me, but by the time I got home, it had disappeared. I supposed it had found its master.

The following morning I went to Bertha's cottage again and once again found her sitting by the fire.

'Well, Bertha,' I said, 'I obeyed you. Last night I was on Arncliffe Bridge.'

'What did you see?'

'Nothing except a slight disturbance of the stream.'

'I know about that, but what else?'

'Nothing.'

'Nothing! Your memory is failing you!'

'Oh, I forgot. On the way home I met a Newfoundland dog belonging to some traveller.'

'That dog never belonged to a mortal,' she said. 'No human is his master. The dog you saw was Barguest. You may have heard of him!'

'I've often heard tales of Barguest but I never believed them. If the old tales are true someone will die after he appears.'

'You are right. And a death will follow last night's appearance.'

'Whose death?'

'Not yours.'

Bertha would tell me no more, so I went home. Less than three hours later I heard that me friend N——, whose figure I had seen in the cauldron steam, had that morning committed suicide by drowning himself at Arncliffe Bridge at the very spot where I saw the disturbance of the stream!

# OLD NANNY

*Nidderdale*

> Come in this minute or Old Nanny will get you!
> Old Nanny overlooked his pigs and they all died!
> Old Nanny'll find you! If you go down there!

Who is Old Nanny/Old Alice/Old Peggy? You may think that she is an old woman living just beyond the end of the village, or that she haunts the crossroads or the churchyard or sits below the gibbet. You may use her to frighten your children away from abandoned houses, or old wells, or even other people's property, but one thing is certain: once you have let her into your mind, she will set up lodgings in your imagination. Then, you had best beware!

One night a farmer living near Stokesley wakes to find Old Nanny standing at the end of his bed. He knows it is her because all the hair on his head is standing on end and his heart is beating fit to bust.

'What do you want?' he gasps.

'Get the gold!' she says. 'Get the silver!'

'I've neither one!' he stammers, though it is a lie.

'Get the gold! Get the silver!'

This time she points out of the window towards the orchard, where the new spring leaves shine in the moonlight as if they are themselves made of silver.

The farmer begins to think that perhaps she has not come to rob him after all.

'Under the foremost!' says Old Nanny. 'Take the silver; leave the gold. Give it to Annie.'

'That dirty old witch who lives just beyond village end? Why her?'

'Give it to Annie!' she repeats. She takes a step backwards, out of the moonlight and is gone.

The farmer lies awake panting and unable to get back to sleep, but as soon as the sun begins rise he leaps from his bed. The farm men yawning and rubbing their eyes as they come into the kitchen are amazed when he strides through them.

'Where's farmer going at sparrow's fart?' mutters one. They all stare out of the back door as the farmer goes first to the cart shed for an old spade and then marches straight towards the orchard.

'Eh! Farmer's crackin'!' they opine gleefully.

The farmer digs under the tree closest to the house, and, just as Old Nanny has said, he unearths a chest of treasure. It is full of silver and gold. He waits until all the men have gone about their work and then brings it into the house. In his room he runs his fingers through the coins. How delightfully heavy they are!

He does not for a moment consider giving anything at all to Annie; lonely, miserable, hungry and cold in her little tumbledown cottage. He thinks, 'The chest was in my orchard, on my land and I dug it up. It's mine!'

But once Old Nanny gets into your mind you're never free again. From the moment he shuts the chest on that decision everything begins to go wrong for him. He does not notice immediately, though he remarks to his surprised foreman on how unseasonably cold it has suddenly become.

That night he wakes to see Old Nanny sitting on a chair by the fire he has had lit in his bedroom. She does not speak, just looks at him. He pretends not to see her and turns over.

The next night she is there again, and the next.

'T'awd bitch'll never wear me down!' the farmer mutters to himself, pulling the blankets over his head.

The next evening he finds himself, uncharacteristically, heading for the alehouse. 'Just a bit of a stiffener,' he tells the surprised land-lord, 'to face her down.' He does not say who 'her' is. The following evening he goes again. Soon it becomes a regular habit. His men increasingly have to go and help bring him home. He often says that Old Nanny is following him, but that he will face her down, t'awd bitch – then he laughs drunkenly. The men look nervously behind them but there is never anyone there.

'Farmer's finally cracked!' they say.

The farmer never sleeps well any more until dawn is near. He rises later and later and stops supervising his men's work. Inevitably they take advantage. The farm starts to go to rack and ruin.

He still rides weekly to Stokesley market but as often as not the horse will have to find its own way home with its owner slumped drunkenly asleep in the saddle.

One wild and windy Saturday night, however, he is not asleep. On the contrary, the villagers are themselves woken by shouting, the clatter of hooves and a terrified neighing. As they throw their shutters open the farmer gallops furiously by, spurring his horse unmercifully. As he passes they hear him shouting 'I will! I will! I will!' Then some see that up behind him is a hunched shape, a small woman in black. She wears the straw hat of an ordinary farm labourer's wife, but she is clinging to the farmer like a cat with her long pointed fingernails.

The farm gate is shut and though the newly awoken men run into the yard at the noise of hooves, they are not fast enough to open it. That does not stop the farmer; he brings his whip down again and again on the horse's flank. 'I will! I will! I will!' he screams.

'He's niver going to leap t'gate!' the men gasp, but, yes, there he goes!

Some of the men try to grab the reins of frightened horse as it lands skidding on the cobblestones, but it rears violently as they approach, throwing off its passengers. The farmer flies through the air and hits his own doorstep with a crack they can all hear. The foreman runs to his side. He kneels down to help him – too late; his master's head is covered with blood, his eyes are open and sightless.

Of Old Nanny there is no sign.

She hasn't gone far though.

She's in your head now …

## The Nine of Hearts

*Swaledale*

George Winterfield was a stealer of hearts. The girls of Leeming, near the River Swale, were attracted by his good looks and easy charm. He was excitingly wild too, known for his drinking and gambling, his jokes, his daring.

He had a girl, promised her marriage, as everyone knew, but somehow there was never quite enough money or the time was not quite right – maybe next year? She waited patiently, but as time wore on, she became increasingly desperate. The other village girls had been jealous when she bagged George, so they were not inclined to be kind to her as the prospect of her marriage appeared to recede indefinitely. George himself remained as friendly and charming to them all as if he was not promised at all.

One evening he was playing cards with his mates in Leeming Mill. George played most winter evenings when there was nothing else to do. The miller's wife brewed a good ale, his fire was warm and the company, for the most part, jolly – unless they were losing, of course. There were four of them: the miller himself, George and two old school friends, John Braithwaite and Tim Farndale. None of them was a rich man, so the pot was not very large, but, even so, George was a canny player with something of a reputation to keep. Occasionally a passing visitor would be invited to join the game, usually going away poorer than he had arrived. When that happened the girls of Leeming would get all sorts of small treats from George; rides at the fair, ribbons, sweetmeats and so on. It will never be known what the poor lass to whom he was promised thought of this.

On this particular evening, the frost was crackling on the windows and the miller's fire was crackling on the broad hearth. The men sat down to their game with pleasure, but something strange happened. George was dealt eight consecutive hands containing the nine of hearts.

All you mathematicians will know that, provided all the cards are properly shuffled, the odds of the next hand also having a nine of hearts in it are the same as for the first. But those who play with the Devil's Picture books are not mathematicians, at least the men at this table were not. To them it seemed impossible that the nine of hearts would turn up for a ninth time.

Tim was so sure he wagered a guinea that it would not. George, who had been losing all night, was not prepared to wager more than a shilling that it would. John opted out. The miller thoughtfully filled their mugs with ale wondering whether he would lay a bet of his own. He looked at the high colours of the others, their bright drunken eyes and shivered unexpectedly, despite the heat. Something was wrong somehow. He glanced around the room where the shadows cast by the leaping fire suddenly seemed ominous. The flickering confused him. For a moment he thought he ... but no, no one was there.

'Come on man! Art thoo in?' He realised that the others were waiting for him. 'Nay, lads, I'll sit this'un out.'

John dealt the cards. George moved to lay his bet.

'Put thy brass in thy pocket,' said a harsh voice, just behind him. Everyone jumped and looked around. Awd Molly stood there, Molly Cass, named locally as a witch by giggling girls. Normally the miller, who did not hold with such foolishness, would have invited her over to the fire for a warm, but her sudden appearance, from nowhere it seemed, filled him with alarm.

'Put thy brass in thy pocket,' she said again to George. 'Thy brass is not for him and his brass is not for thee.' So great was her reputation for ferocity, that neither George nor Tim dared disobey her. They pocketed

their money. Molly moved forwards to the table and stared hard at the backs of George's cards, which lay there still unexamined.

'George, thoo's got it again. The nine. Tek up thy hand and see.'

George shrugged with an affectation of carelessness and picked up his cards. There, shining as red as drops of blood, was the ninth nine of hearts.

'George, thoo's hit it eight times already and the Old 'Un (the Devil) is in thee now. He'll not leave thee till he's got thee altogether! Thoo's thrown away thy chance, so I've pitched it into the Swale. Now the Swale's waiting for thee, George. It's going to be thy bridal bed!'

The others stared at George whose ruddy face had paled. He forced a laugh. 'What's thoo blethering about Awd Molly? I've not thrown away any chance.'

'Where is thy bride?'

George froze at the words. He knew that he had not treated Mary well, that he had been faithless, careless of her happiness and occasionally really cruel. Had something happened to her?

'I'll make it up to her. I'll wed her straight away. Give me another chance.'

'I'm not often in the mind to give one chance, let alone two. Go thy gate. Thy bride's waiting for thee in a bed of bulrushes. Oh, what a bridal bed!'

George staggered to his feet, knocking over his chair. He stumbled past Awd Molly and through the door.

'Good night, George!' Molly cried after him. 'All roads lead to the Swale tonight!'

His friends heard him crashing down the stairs and slamming the outside door behind him. Awd Molly hawked and spat scornfully into the fire. Then without a word, she turned and followed George downstairs.

When the miller heard the banging on his door the following morning he knew without being told that the news was bad. Sure enough, a carter bringing oats to the mill had seen something at the edge of the River Swale. He climbed from the cart to investigate. Lying together in a muddy bed of bulrushes were George and his poor Mary. The carter called for help but it was too late; they were both drowned and cold.

Had they met? Had she drowned herself first? Had his guilt led him to follow her? Had he murdered her and then committed suicide? There were no answers. Awd Molly might have had some but she held her peace and no one dared ask her.

Dales folk say that if you are brave enough to walk by the Swale at midnight you will see them in the water sometimes; first the girl, then the man, their pale bloated bodies drifting with the flow, slowly moving closer together.


## OLD MOLLY AND THE CAUL

A lass if born in June with a caul
Will wed, hev bairns & rear 'em all.
But a lass if born with a caul in July,
Will loose her caul & her young will die.
Every month beside luck comes with a caul
If safe put by,
If lost she may cry:
For ill luck on her will fall.
For man it's luck – be born when he may –
It is safe be kept ye mind,
But if lost it be he'll find
Ill-deed his lot for many a day.

(Fairfax-Blakeborough, 1923)

A baby born with a caul, or mask, over the face is lucky as long as the caul is kept safe. Such a baby will never drown and will grow up able to do many things that an ordinary person cannot – as long as they do not lose it. But the caul's power is coveted by witches who are always trying to steal them.

Jane Herd was born with a caul of particular power. If she laid it on the Bible and spoke a name, that person was bound to come to see her shortly afterwards. Many were the strange things that she could do, but, being a churchgoing lass, she never used her caul for ill.

One day when she was using the caul she had the window open and a chance gust of wind blew it right out and away. Jane rushed to catch it but it was so light that she did not know in which direction it had been blown and so it was lost.

From that day on Jane's luck turned. Her betrothed cancelled their marriage, she developed a nasty lump on her neck and her right knee began to hurt so badly that she could barely walk. People began to speculate as to what was causing the trouble and the consensus was that some evil person had hold of the caul and was using it to curse her.

The only person Jane could remember seeing in the street on the day her caul disappeared was Molly Cass, but she had been so far away that it seemed impossible that she could be the culprit. There was only one thing for it – she would have to consult the wise men of Bedale. Master Sadler and Thomas Spence had great names in those days as healers and solvers of uncanny problems. No doubt there was a doctor somewhere in the neighbourhood, but doctors were expensive and not really trusted by local people. No, it was the wise men that would have the answer.

Nervously Jane went to see them. They made mystic signs around the lump and the bad knee. Then they told her of certain secret ingredients she was to bring to them at midnight the following evening.

When she arrived at the appointed time, a fire of wickenwood (rowan, the sovereign against witches) had been kindled on their hearth and the ingredients she had brought were solemnly boiled together in a great pot, which she had to stir with a wickenwood rod until a thick black smoke began to rise from it. Jane was told to inhale the smoke nine times; coughing and retching she did her best. Then, still holding the rod, she had to place her other hand on the Bible and repeat the following question: 'Has —— got ma caul?' (Inserting the name of anyone she suspected.) After a minute Master Sadler said, 'No, she is free!' and Jane had to go on to name another suspect.

Name after name she suggested with no result, but the moment she mentioned Molly Cass the pot boiled over and there was such a terrible smoke and stench that they all had to run into the backyard. There they disturbed Molly herself, standing on a settle and peering through a crack in the shutters! They all three grabbed her and forced her into the smoke-filled room. She coughed and shouted and wheezed, but to save herself from suffocation she was finally forced to confess that she had the caul. Gasping she promised to return it.

Jane was not very forgiving. She and the wise men locked Molly
in the stable with a wickenwood peg fastening the door so that she
could not break out. The next day she was ducked nine times in
the mill race.

For sure she was a queer awd lass
As mean as muck, as bold as brass.
I mean t'awd witch, awd Molly Cass
At lived nigh t'mill at Leeming.

# ABOUT MOTHER SHIPTON

*Nidderdale*

Close to the Dropping Well in Knaresborough is a small gloomy cave said to have been the birthplace and home of the famous prophetess, Mother Shipton. Both cave and well have probably been regarded as sacred for many hundreds of years, but she herself appeared on the scene much more recently, probably in the seventeenth century, when the earliest mention of her can be found in chapbooks.

Celia Fiennes, an early tourist in North Yorkshire, wrote a description of the Dropping Well in the 1690s, but failed to mention Mother Shipton, so it seems her fame had not yet become widespread. Celia had clearly not read the version of Mother Shipton's life and prophesies by one Richard Head (1684), which, complete with a description of her hideousness and an imaginative sixteenth-century back-story, was about to become the generally accepted orthodoxy.

It may be that his version is based on folk memories of a real person, but no evidence for her existence has ever been found. However, by the eighteenth century, Head's account of Ursula Southeil, the hideous but gifted seeress who married a Mr Shipton and prophesied the downfall of Cardinal Wolsey, was firmly ensconced in the public imagination, her prophesies conveniently proved true by all being about events in the past.

Real people sometimes become legends, but imaginary people can also sometimes acquire the status of reality. People wanted Mother Shipton to exist, and so exist she did – and still does, at least in the popular imagination. She has certainly enhanced Knaresborough's tourist credentials over the centuries. In the xenophobic eighteenth century, Mother Shipton's big advantage was that she was English, unlike Nostradamus – a genuine visionary – whose prophesies her own were said to rival.

Subsequent editors of Mother Shipton's prophesies could not resist the opportunity of inventing new ones, all intended to 'foretell' topical events of the day. Charles Hindley, for example, admitted that he had added some verses in his 1862 edition, including a supposed prophesy of the Crystal Palace and the Crimean War:

A house of glass shall come to pass
In England, but alas,
War will follow with the work
In the land of the pagan and the Turk.

Whatever Mother Shipton's existential status, she remains one of Knaresborough's important tourist attractions, and a visit to her cave and the Dropping Well an interesting, if expensive, experience.

There are many stories told of her but my favourite is the one that follows.

## MOTHER SHIPTON TEACHES A LESSON

Mother Shipton had become such a celebrity in Knaresborough that people would not leave her alone. She could not stick her long warty nose out of doors without a crowd gathering around her asking ill-mannered questions.

Finally, she could bear it no longer. 'Time to teach them a lesson,' she thought.

One of her neighbours, a rich man of the town with a fine house, had invited some local bigwigs to a breakfast party. Mother Shipton watched them in her magic mirror, muttering under her breath.

The party got off to a good start. The tables were laden with chops, steaks, eggs, ham and all the things that the wealthy used to eat for breakfast in those days. The guests seemed to get on well. They ate, drank and chatted merrily. After a while, however, the atmosphere began to get more hectic. One man began to laugh loudly. When asked what the joke was, he pointed to the dignified old gentleman sitting opposite him. Instead of a ruff he appeared suddenly to be wearing a necklace of juicy pork faggots! Everyone began to laugh at him as well, but the first man's smile was wiped off his face when his hat was whisked off and replaced by a pewter chamber pot. His frantic efforts to remove it made the young lady opposite him laugh so much that she nearly split her stays. Unfortunately for her she soon found that she could not stop laughing but was forced to continue, getting redder and redder. How infectious laughter is! Soon the whole company was laughing so uncontrollably that the tears poured down their cheeks.

The master of the house, who had been in the kitchen getting more ham, came running to see what was causing the hilarity. As he got to the door, he was stopped by a violent blow on the head. Feeling his head with his hands he discovered, with a gasp of horror, that he appeared to have grown a pair of cuckold's horns so enormous that no matter how hard he tried he could not get them through the door. The effect on his guests was predictable; they were now cackling so hard that some of them actually rolled off their chairs onto the floor, sweaty-faced and howling with merriment.

Now Mother Shipton, sitting in her cave, clapped her hands. Instantly all laughter at the party ceased as if it had been turned off. Hilarity was replaced by total silence. Suddenly no one felt in the least amused. A moment later, they heard the noise of mocking laughter begin again but it was not theirs. They looked around; there was no one in the room but themselves. A hundred invisible people appeared to be finding them hysterically amusing.

Now the guests became frightened. Muttering excuses to their host, they called for their horses and began to run down the stairs to the courtyard. The magic followed them; hard little apples began to pelt them, thrown by invisible hands. The horses were brought, neighing and kicking, by frightened servants. The guests quickly mounted up but their troubles were not yet over for the moment they settled in their saddles ugly little women appeared behind each one, sitting on their cruppers and holding whips in their hands. With these, the women beat the horses so fiercely that they galloped home as though the Devil himself were after them.

No one was hurt, but all were very angry. It did not take them long to work out who to blame.

'It was the magic of Mother Shipton! We want her summoned to answer for her witchcraft!' they shouted at the local magistrates.

The punishment for witchcraft in England in those days was death – not by burning (that was only done in Scotland) but by hanging. Still, death by any method is to be avoided!

Mother Shipton was summoned before the magistrates and duly appeared. She did not deny her responsibility for the strange happenings, but said that she had merely been demonstrating what it was like to be the subject of continual jokes, insults and unwelcome attention.

'Just leave me alone or I'll do it again!' she threatened.

What judgement the magistrates would have passed on her will never be known, for at that moment she suddenly got bored with the whole thing and cried out at the top of her voice, 'Updraxi, call Stygician Helluei!' whereupon a dragon flew through the window and carried her away in a clap of thunder …

# 8

# York Stories

York stories could fill a book on their own, especially if you add all the ghost stories for which the town is famous. Here are a selection, starting with one of the oldest.

## Ragnar Lodbrok and the Founding of York

There was a man living in Denmark called Ragnar. He was big and strong, a great warrior.

There was a powerful king of Denmark called Herrud who had a very beautiful daughter called Thora Fortress-Hart.

One day Herrud gave his daughter a little jewelled snake. He used to give her a present every day because he loved her so much. He had made her a beautiful bower to live in surrounded by a fence. Thora liked the snake and put it in a small box on top of a piece of gold. Next day both the snake and the gold had grown a little; a month later, the snake and the gold had grown a great deal. Soon the snake was too big for the box but curled around it. It went on growing. Eventually it grew so large that it was too big for the bower and it lay encircling it, with its tail in its mouth. The pile of gold on which it slept was huge. Now it became very difficult to deal with as it ate an ox a day and threatened harm to anyone who wanted to go into the bower, except for Thora. People were afraid of it because it had become very poisonous.

The king declared that whoever killed the serpent would marry his daughter and get the big pile of gold as her dowry.

Ragnar heard about this. He had shaggy, hairy clothes made, breeches and a cape. He boiled them in tar. That summer he sailed to the place where King Herrud's hall stood. He put on the shaggy clothes and rolled on the beach until he was covered all over with sand. Then he went to find the serpent and they fought together. The serpent fought fiercely but it could not bite through the shaggy tarry garments and the sand hurt its mouth. In the end, Ragnar was able to stab it with his spear. The serpent's boiling poisonous blood spouted out and hit him between the shoulderblades, but the clothes protected him from all harm.

This was how he acquired the name Ragnar Lodbrok (meaning hairy breeches).

King Herrud was very pleased to find such a good warrior. He was happy to honour his promise and so Ragnar married Thora, and received all of the serpent gold. He began to have a great name all around Denmark. His fame even reached as far as England. The gold attracted many warriors to join his war-band.

When the couple had been happily married for some time and had two sons, Thora fell ill and died and Ragnar grieved for her.

There was a beautiful woman called Aslaug. She was the daughter of Sigurd Dragon'sbane and Brynhild the Valkyrie. She was the wisest woman of her day. Ragnar married her and they had five sons. They were called Ivarr the Boneless, Bjorn Ironsides, Hvitserk the Swift, Rognvald and Sigurd Snake-in-the-eye. They grew into fine warriors; as soon as they could wield swords they went off with their men to win gold and conquer towns as far away as Italy. It is said that they even wanted to conquer Rome, but decided the distance was too great.

There was a king called Aelle, who ruled the part of Britain called Northumbria, which in those days ran from the Humber all the way to Scotland. He had a stronghold at Crayke.

Ragnar spent his summers raiding and harrying all around Scandinavia, but when he heard how famous his sons were becoming he grew jealous. He began to pour a huge amount of money into building and fitting out two large transport ships. People realised that he must be planning a big war expedition.

'What are those ships for?' asked Aslaug.

'I have harried in many places but never in England, which is very rich. Those ships will carry all my men there,' replied Ragnar.

'I think it would be more sensible to have smaller ships because they are less likely to be wrecked. The coast of England is treacherous.'

'No one has ever conquered England with just two ships,' he objected, 'I'll be all the more famous if I pull it off.'

'You won't be famous if all your men are drowned or lose their weapons in the sea, because then the king of that land will very quickly beat you. Longships are much easier to steer into harbour and they're cheaper.'

'I have never known a pile of gold protect anyone when his enemies were at the gates,' he retorted, 'I shall spend my money as I please!'

'Hmm!' said Aslaug. She went away and began to weave a magic shirt for him.

The ships were at last ready. Ragnar's gold attracted many men to sail with him.

On the day they departed, Aslaug came to bid them farewell. She gave Ragnar the shirt. 'I have woven this shirt from grey hair,' she said, 'it will protect you from all wounds. Please wear it for my sake.'

Ragnar thanked her gratefully. She was only ever known to have shed one tear. It was when her stepsons were killed – and it had been red and hard as a hailstone, but people around them could see that she was deeply unhappy as the ships rowed away. Some thought it a bad omen.

As she had predicted, Ragnar's ships were wrecked in storms on the coast of Yorkshire (then part of Northumbria). Fortunately, however, none of the men drowned and they all managed to keep hold of their weapons. Once they were all gathered together again, they set off to raid towns and villages.

King Aelle had already been warned about Ragnar's sailing from Denmark. He had assembled a great host. Now he spoke to them: 'Make sure that you do not kill old Hairy Breeches. Try to work out which one he is and then capture him. He has five fierce sons who will not spare any of us if we kill him!'

Ragnar and his men prepared for battle. He wore Aslaug's shirt over his mail and had his great serpent-killing spear in his hand.

The two hosts came together, but Ragnar's was much smaller than Aelle's. Ragnar did great deeds of arms, slaughtering many of Aelle's best men, but in the end, his army was destroyed. He himself fought so well that no one would attack him anymore, but pressed him down with shields so that he could be captured.

The men brought their prisoner before the king in Crayke, saying that he refused to say who he was. Aelle thought he was probably Ragnar, but he could not be sure.

'We will put him in the snake pit until he tells us his name. We can easily take him out again if he really is Ragnar.'

They dragged him away and threw him into the pit. The snakes did not bite him and he sat there in the dark for a long time. The king's men were worried.

'This is a mighty man,' they said. 'No one could wound him in battle and now the snakes won't dare bite him!'

They went and told the king. Aelle said, 'There is some sorcery here. Take off his clothes and then we'll see.'

They stripped Ragnar and put him back in the pit. This time the snakes fastened themselves onto him greedily. Ragnar said, 'The piglets would grunt now if they knew what the old pig suffers!' The men on guard did not understand what he was talking about. Then he said, 'I have fought in fifty-one battles, a good tally, and have slaughtered many men, but I never guessed that I would be killed by a snake! What a joke!'

He began to grow weaker. After a little while, he said again, 'The piglets would grunt now if they knew what the old pig suffers!' Then he lay down and died.

When King Aelle heard his words he knew beyond doubt that it was Ragnar he had killed.

'We must handle the piglets carefully!' he said. 'Let us see whether a trough full of gold will stop their squealing.'

He prepared to send messengers to Ragnar's sons.

## IVARR'S REVENGE

King Aelle told his messengers, 'Watch carefully how each of the sons takes the news of his father's death. I want to see which of them is the most dangerous.'

One of Ragnar's sons had been killed in Italy, but the surviving four had returned to Denmark some time before this. They were entertaining themselves in various ways when Aelle's messengers arrived. Ivarr sat in the high seat; Sigurd Snake-in-the-eye and Hvitserk the Swift were playing chess; Bjorn Ironsides was fitting a spearhead to a shaft.

The leader of the messengers related the story of Ragnar's death without omitting any details. When he got to the part where Ragnar said 'The piglets would grunt', Bjorn's hand clenched the spearshaft so hard that he left his handprint on it. Hvitserk gripped a chess piece he had just taken so violently that blood spurted out from under every nail. Sigurd was paring his nails with a knife and cut his finger to the bone, without noticing. Ivarr quietly asked a few questions, though his face went red and then black and then deathly pale. The messengers could see that his very skin was swelling with anger, but he spoke politely to them and sent them away with gifts.

When King Aelle heard what the messengers had to say he thought about it for a while. Then he said, 'Ivarr is the only one we need to fear. We should be able to defeat the others easily.' And he set a watch on his kingdom.

Ragnar's sons held a council. Ivarr took the lead and stated, 'I'm going to accept compensation from Aelle. Our father was far too reckless. He had no reason to invade England.'

The others were angry with him because they wanted to take revenge. 'We will never take money for our father.'

'Well, we shall see what will happen,' retorted Ivarr. 'I shall go to Aelle and see what he offers me. You three can rule Denmark, but be sure to send me money when I ask you.' Though they were not happy, they agreed to that.

Ivarr crossed the sea and presented himself before King Aelle.

'I have come to discuss compensation for my father,' he said, 'I don't see why we can't settle this amicably.'

'Some men say that you say one thing and do another,' replied the king. 'How do I know that I can trust you?'

'The proof of the pudding is in the eating,' replied Ivarr. 'I shall not ask a great deal and I will swear never to oppose you.'

The king could not see any flaws in this, so he asked what compensation Ivarr wanted.

'As much of your land as an ox-hide can cover. I shall build on that.'

Aelle said, 'That will not harm the kingdom. I agree providing you take an oath never to fight against me.' This was done.

Ivarr took an old ox-hide, soaked it and stretched it. Then he split the flesh side from the hairy side and cut each into a very thin, long thong. When they were stretched out, they enclosed enough land to build a town on. Ivarr got carpenters and had them build houses. He called the town York, or Eoforwick, the Town of the Boar, remembering his father's last words, and many people came to live there. Ivarr became very well thought of because he was generous and always gave good advice. King Aelle received much help from him in battle as well as in the running of the country. He began to trust him and gave him important tasks.

Ivarr sent messages to his brothers asking for lots of gold and silver. They were curious but realised that he had some plan they did not know about. They sent him all he asked for.

When the money arrived, Ivarr began giving great presents to the most important men in the kingdom. Soon he had persuaded many of King Aelle's best fighting men to swear that they would stay at home if the king went to war.

The following summer he secretly summoned his brothers to raise levies and come over to Northumbria with as large an army as they could get.

Soon King Aelle heard that Ragnar's sons were coming against him. He tried to summon his own levies but few came. He asked Ivarr what he should do.

'Let me go and meet my brothers,' said Ivarr, 'it may be that I will be able to stop them advancing any further'.

He went to see his brothers. 'Advance as quickly as you can!' he told them. 'The king's army is much smaller than yours.'

'Don't teach your granny to suck eggs!' they replied.

When Ivarr came back to King Aelle he shook his head sadly. 'I'm afraid that my brothers are far too angry and revengeful to sign any truce. When I tried to suggest it, they howled like wolves! I shall not fight you, as I have sworn not to, but I won't fight against my brothers either. Good luck!'

King Aelle marched with his army against the sons of Ragnar, but they were so filled with fury that they cut through the ranks of his men like a knife through butter. The army fled and King Aelle was captured. He was dragged before Ivarr and the other sons.

'Now you can see that the piglets have tusks!' said Ivarr to him. 'We shall fill our troughs with your blood!' He ordered the blood eagle to be cut on Aelle's back so that he died in agony after a long time. Then Ivarr took over the kingdom of Northumberland and ruled it from York for a long time.

Thus, the sons of Ragnar Lodbrok took their revenge on his killer.


## BROTHER JOCUNDUS

Whether Brother Jocundus was the worst monk ever I am not sure, but he was certainly ill-suited to his calling. For a start, he loved food more than was strictly proper; he also enjoyed a merry song, a bit of a dance, a mug of strong ale, a saucy joke and a pretty – but enough!

In those days, York was a city of churches and monasteries. St Leonards Priory, where Brother Jocundus was a monk, was situated, so the story says, right slap next to the great Abbey of St Mary, famous for its good living and rich endowments. St Leonard's was much poorer and rather austere – not ideal for a jolly soul such as Brother Jocundus!

One day he was sitting in his little cell looking gloomy. He was supposed to be meditating on the scriptures but the noise of music and merriment floating in through the window was proving something of a distraction. He knew all too well what it was: the sound of the St Bartholomew's Day Fair.

'There will be stalls with sausages and pies and oysters and ale and sweetmeats and gingerbread and –' he thought, '… games and races and bearded ladies and tumblers and merry Andrews and merry-go-rounds and freaks and seesaws!'

He sighed and tried harder to concentrate on the Lamentations of Isaiah, but it was no good. Two minutes later, after hearing a particularly loud burst of 'Belle qui tien ma vie' played on the sackbut, he slammed his Bible shut and leapt to his feet.

'St Leonard forgive me, but I have to get out of here!'

He opened the door, and peered around. Everyone seemed to be safely studying in their cells. He crept out and down to the porter's little cubby hole. He was in luck; the porter was having an after-dinner snooze. He was just about to creep on when he remembered something that threatened to spoil his afternoon: he had no money.

'Well, might as well be hanged for a sheep as a lamb!' he thought and grabbed the poor-box that stood on a table near the door. Then he was gone out into the busy crowded street.

What joys awaited him! Bootham was crowded with all the things he had imagined – and more. There were jugglers who tossed flaming brands in a bright circle about their heads; there were sword-swallowers and fire-eaters; there were contortionists whose writhing made his eyes water. Some people were doing a long dance to bagpipes, up and down the street. In one place, there was a crowd around a couple of slippery, straining, grunting wrestlers. In another people were cheering a boy trying to climb a well-greased pole at the top of which was tied a squealing piglet.

Brother Jocundus strolled through the throng watching and laughing, his hands full of pies and sausages. His poor-box money did not last long, but he found, to his amazement, that folk were so amused to see a portly monk enjoying himself out of his cloister that they bought him things just to see him eat them. Soon, since he did not seem averse to it, some troublemakers started buying him drink as well.

'What do you think of this?' they asked him.

He tried new ale, old ale, spiced ale, cock ale, mead, metheglyn, malmsey and the special St Bartholomew's Strong Feast ale. Then, just as he was beginning to think he should get back to his monastery and wondering vaguely where it was, he saw the seesaw.

It was not like the pathetic ones you still occasionally find in children's playgrounds, it was a *proper* one: a ten-foot plank (no handles) balanced over a barrel. The idea was to try to dislodge the person sitting at the other end. Now, it so happened that Brother Jocundus had excelled at this when he was a boy and when some of his new drinking companions suggested that he have a go, he forgot about the dignity of holy orders and jumped at the chance. Soon he was whizzing through the air singing 'In dulci jubilo-o-o, Up-up-up I go-o-o!' Then he hit the ground with a

bone-shattering crash and rolled off singing 'Do-ow-own I go-o-o!'
He lay on the ground giggling helplessly.

Suddenly the laughter around him ceased. Brother Jocundus did
not notice, but people were falling back and bowing respectfully.
A nearby bagpipe gave a dying wail and fell silent. There stood the
Prior of St Leonard's, surrounded by monks, his face like thunder.
Brother Jocundus peered at the prior. 'Hello Father, want a go?'
he began, but before he could say any more, brawny monkish arms
had seized him and started carrying him back to the monastery.
He lay back happily and continued singing.

The prior was so infuriated by Brother Jocundus' behaviour that
he called a hasty council of older monks to decide on a suitable
punishment. They decided that the only one severe enough was for
him to be walled up in the cellar.

'Only right for one who has insulted our monastery by behaving
like a drunken tinker!'

Brother Jocundus was still as drunk as a lord and was affection-
ately telling the prior that he was his very bes' mate as they laid him
on the ground in a handy cellar room and began walling him in.
One monk, kinder than the rest, put a jug of water and a loaf of
bread beside him as, to the sound of prayers and the clinking of
trowels, the wall slowly grew upwards. The last thing the monks
heard from Brother Jocundus as they trooped up the cellar stairs
was a fading 'In dulci jubilo-o-o' that ended in a long snore.

He woke in the dark with a raging headache and a terrible thirst.
He thought he was in his cell, but when he flailed around with his
arms, he realised that it had shrunk. Why was he on the ground? He
found the jug of water and drank, but as alcohol receded, fear took
its place. Had he gone blind? Had he 'died' and been buried alive?
He struck out in terror. Some stones in the wall on his left moved.
Filled with a sudden desperation born of terror and hope, he hit
and kicked the wall as hard as he could. A stone fell out and light
leaked in. With a mighty heave he forced a hole in the wall and
squeezed through in a flurry of mortar. He looked around. He was
in a cellar, but not one he recognised. He shook the dust off his robe
and stood up. Cautiously he crept past rows of barrels towards the

light of the staircase. At the top, he heard a familiar sound; the slapping of monkish sandals as brothers headed towards the monastery church for a service. Pulling his cowl down over his face, he nipped out of the doorway and joined the end of the line.

And that was how Brother Jocundus unintentionally joined the monastery of St Mary's.

Monks are not encouraged to speak and though a few puzzled eyebrows were raised, no one wasted precious words questioning him. He joined in the usual tasks, though he found he had to work harder at St Mary's as it was a much bigger monastery. Despite what he had heard about its rich food, it seemed that ordinary monks did not see much of it. After a year, he was both fitter and leaner.

His brush with death meant that he was so worried about being caught again he became a model monk, but it was this obedience that brought him to the attention of the abbot.

One day he was summoned to the abbot's room.

'Well, Brother – John, is it?'

'Yes, your reverence.'

'Brother John, I have noticed that you seem a very modest hard-working monk.'

Brother Jocundus looked modestly at his feet.

'And so, as Brother James has unfortunately left us to take his heavenly reward, I have decided to make you my cellarer in his place.'

Brother Jocundus stared at him in shock. 'But–'

'No need to thank me! Just make sure that my valuable wines are well kept. That is all.'

Poor Brother Jocundus! It was a sentence almost as cruel as being walled up, because the abbot's cellar was famous. Even the king had been known to visit him unexpectedly just to sample his old burgundy. A cellar full of delicate wines, just sitting there slowly maturing! They sat in their casks, smiling coquettishly at Brother Jocundus, saying 'Drink me! Drink me!' With a tremendous effort, he withstood their temptations …

Until …

One day the abbot sent for Brother Jocundus and told him that he wanted a very special wine sent up for dinner. He was entertaining some important French merchants and wanted to show them that he knew his wines.

'Which wine, my lord Abbot?'

'The old malmsey in the little cask. It should be just right now. Send up a silver jug of it when you hear grace being sung. The big silver jug, mind you, well scoured. Not a pottery one'.

Brother Jocundus went down into the cellar and soon found the little cask. As was his job, he broached it and hammered in a tap. A very little of it leaked out onto his fingers. He licked it off. 'Oh, that's nice! That's very nice! Well, I've been a good boy for a whole year now. It's time I had a tiny treat!' He poured a small bowl of the malmsey and drank it off, smacking his lips.

The abbot sat uncomfortably between his two well-upholstered guests making frantic but silent signs with his eyebrows to the monk who was serving him. The monk leaned closer. 'Where's the wine?' hissed the abbot out of the side of his mouth. The monk bowed and disappeared downstairs.

'I promise that it'll be worth wait when it comes!' blustered the abbot.

His guests shrugged. 'Nous verrons!' they said. But they never did!

When the serving monk reached the top of the cellar steps he could hear an unholy sound. Somebody was singing.

'In dulci jubilo-o-o! Up-up-up we go-o-o!' Brother Jocundus lay beneath the little cask, alternating between singing lustily and catching the last drops of wine on his tongue.

Only one punishment was severe enough for such a betrayal of trust. The abbot decreed that the vile monk should be walled up in the very cellar he had so desecrated. A convenient hole in the wall was discovered with what seemed like an old pantry behind it. Brother Jocundus was unceremoniously pushed into it. A compassionate monk put a loaf of bread hot from the oven and a jug of milk into the hole with him; then he was walled-up and once more left in the dark.

Now it so happened that the prior of St Leonard's had died a few days before and his funeral had just come to an end. All the monks were about to gather to choose a new prior when someone had the bright idea that a jug of wine might help with their deliberations.

As the cellarer was bending over a cask, he heard a sound that froze the blood in his veins.

'In dulci jubilo-o-o …'

The cellarer ran, wine splashing from the jug. 'Help! Ghost!' he cried as he ran. 'Ghost! The undead!' His brother monks gathered around.

'Brother Jocundus' ghost is haunting the cellar! I heard him! Singing *that* song!'

They told him not to be silly, patted him on the back and implied that he had been sampling the cellar's contents. 'No I haven't!' he wept. 'Come and hear for yourself. It's Brother Jocundus!'

Laughing, they accompanied him down into the cellar, but the smiles were quickly wiped off their faces. 'In dulci jubilo-o-o!' came loud and clear from the other side of the wall. The monks stared at each other wondering what to do. Then one, more organised than the others, ran for a pickaxe. In a short time, the wall was broken down. There lay Brother Jocundus, smiling and waving vaguely.

'He's still alive! After a year!'

'He looks well – in better shape than ever!'

One monk reached into the hole and brought out a loaf of bread. 'And the bread's not stale! In fact it's still warm!'

'And the water has been changed into milk!'

'It's a miracle!'

When Brother Jocundus' eyes got used to the light, he saw before him a row of kneeling monks. 'Bless us, O Holy Brother Jocundus!' they chorused.

And that is how he came to be chosen as the new prior of St Leonards!

I don't think he was the holiest prior St Leonard's ever knew, but, with a cellar every bit the rival of St Mary's, he was certainly the jolliest that ever held the office!


## THE BOOK OF FATE

A knight of York is riding home through the city. He is feeling very happy because although (being a knight) he prefers fighting and hunting to reading, he has just fulfilled a secret boyhood dream: he has hunted down a book he has wanted to own since his old tutor told him of it – the *Book of Fate*. It has cost him a great deal of money but, at last, it is his.

Now, this is no ordinary book and it actually requires very little reading because it is magic. Anyone who owns it can see into the future. All you have to do is to write the name of someone on the middle page, close the book, tap it three times, say the magic word (which is a secret) and when you open the book again, there you will find the person's future neatly written.

The knight is leaning back in his saddle feeling unusually benevolent when his eye falls upon a miserable man sitting in the doorway of a little shop. He has his head in his hands and is rocking backwards and forwards saying, 'What are we going to do? What are we going to do?' The knight, who would not normally even notice the man, reins in his grey stallion and leans down.

'You there! What are you wailing about?'

The man looks up with tears in his eyes. 'Oh, sir, my wife has just given birth to another girl!'

'Well, don't despair, she may have a boy next time!' says the knight. The man looks uncomfortable.

'It isn't that she's a girl, my lord, it's that we already have five children and can't afford to feed any more! The poor little thing will starve.'

The knight is about to throw the man some small change when he remembers his new book. He has not tried it out yet. 'Perhaps her future isn't as dark as you think,' he says, 'Wouldn't you like to find out what it's going to be? I have here the famous *Book of Fate*, of which you may have heard. Bring her out and I will tell her fortune!'

Now the man is frightened, but he does not dare argue with the knight – especially as he seems to be a magician as well. He goes into his little shop and after a time comes out again with a tiny bundle in his arms. The knight glances at the baby who screws up her face and howls. He carefully gets out his book and unwraps it from its silken cloth. He is really quite excited. 'What is her name?' he asks.

'Alice Sidebottom,' says the man. (All girls are called Alice in the Middle Ages.) The knight opens the book to the middle page and writes down the name. Then he closes the book, taps it three times and says the magic word (which is *still* secret). Then, his hands shaking a little, he opens the book again. Sure enough, there is some writing that was not there before. The knight reads it and reads it again. The smile fades from his face, which begins to grow red with anger. This is what he has just read: 'Little Alice will marry your son!'

He has to think quickly because the father is looking at him hopefully.

'Ah, hmm, yes, it says that your daughter will - er - be adopted by a knight!' he stammers.

The man's eyes widen. 'Will she, my lord? How wonderful! Wait till I tell my wife!' and he is turning to go into the shop when the knight stops him.

'Yes, and do you know, I've taken such a shine to the little lass that I'd like that knight to be me. Just what I need; I've not got any girls, only boys. She'll want for nothing, marry a lord, eat three meals a day, have rings and all that stuff,' he says. 'Just hand her over and I'll be on my way.'

Well, the man and his wife are delighted – their daughter will now have a far better life than they could provide. The mother puts the baby in a little wooden box to act as a carry-cot and kisses it goodbye. She cries a little as she hands the baby up to the knight. 'Look after her well, my lord,' she says. The knight waves to them gaily as he rides off down the street with baby Alice in her little box tucked under his arm.

When he gets to the bridge over the River Ouze, he pauses. 'No son of mine is going to marry a Sidebottom!' he snarls, tosses the box and its contents over the parapet and spurs his horse forward.

Sixteen years later, the same knight is once more returning home, along the river, this time, with a group of his friends. They have been hunting and are all in a jolly mood. As they approach a humble cottage that stands a little way back from the river bank, the knight suddenly pulls his horse up. 'God's bones!' he exclaims. 'My wife wants to feast you all tonight and I've forgotten the fine fish I promised to bring her.'

'But isn't this is a fisherman's cottage?' says one of his friends. 'Why don't you try here?'

The knight leaps off his horse and bangs loudly on the door. To his surprise, it is opened by a very pretty girl who curtsies politely and asks him whether he would like to buy some fish. The knight and his friends are greatly taken with her. They talk and joke with her, and tease her to make her blush.

'Well, my pretty,' the knight says, curling his moustache, 'I'll certainly buy that big fish I see there on the table, but tell me, wouldn't you like to know your fortune?'

'My father tells me that my face is my only fortune,' the lass replies.

'And a very pretty face it is. But I have here a certain way of discovering your real fortune,' the knight insists, 'For I have here the *Book of Fate*, which is never wrong!' He unwraps the book – which he carries everywhere with him – and shows it to the girl. (His friends stifle a sigh.)

The girl is a little nervous, fearing that the book is evil witchcraft, but in the end she cannot resist the fascination of knowing her fortune.

'What is your name, maiden?'

'Alice Fish, my lord.' (I told you all girls were called Alice in the Middle Ages.)

The knight opens the book at the middle and writes Alice's name in it. Then he closes the book, taps it three times and says the magic word (never to be revealed). Then he opens the book and looks at what is written there:

'Even though you tried to drown her, she is *still* going to marry your son!'

Immediately the knight is shaken with a bout of coughing and spluttering.

Alice looks worried and brings him a cup of water. 'Is my fortune so very dreadful?' she asks. The knight gets some sort of grip on himself.

'No, it's wonderful. You'll marry a nice young fisherman and have fourteen children. Must go feast. Goodbye!'

Then he jumps on his horse and gallops away, followed by his rather confused friends.

They have not gone far along the river before the knight thinks better of his action. A cunning plan is beginning to form itself in his mind.

'Damn me if I haven't left the fish behind!' he tells his friends. 'You go on to York Castle and I'll catch up with you in a minute.' Then he rides back to the cottage. The girl comes rushing out. 'My lord, you forgot your fish!' she cries, holding up a large parcel.

'Thank you, sweetheart,' he says, smiling kindly. 'Do you know, I'm so busy worrying about a problem I have that I'll forget my own head next!'

'What problem's that?' says Alice, who is a very kind, sympathetic sort of girl.

'Well, I have to get an urgent message to my brother in Scarborough Castle and I don't seem to be able to find anyone to take it for me. I don't suppose you know of anyone?' He smiles even more kindly.

Alice thinks for a moment. 'Scarborough Castle is an awful long way away,' she says, 'but I suppose I could take it, when my father comes back. It'd take me more than a day to get there, though.'

'Would you? Would you really? How very sweet you are! Don't worry about money for your journey. Look! Here's a gold noble for food and lodging.' And almost before she realises that she's agreed to go, Alice is watching the knight sitting at her father's table writing a letter. He seals it with his ring and gives it to her. 'Now you really mustn't read it.' he says, laughing.

'Oh, that's all right. I can't read,' she replies.

'Good! Good! Give it into the hand of my brother Sir William as soon as you can. Well, I must go off with the fish before the fish goes off by itself!' He laughs heartily and rides away as quickly as he can.

Alice's father is impressed by the gold noble. 'You'll never need all that. Don't forget to bring the change back with you,' he says as he waves her goodbye with a fishy hand.

Alice is a good walker and enjoys being able to stroll along the highway without any work to do, for though her parents are kind folk, they are not rich and she still has to work hard cleaning fish or carrying them to market.

A kindly carter gives her a lift for a bit of the way, but night draws near long before she gets to Scarborough. Alice looks around for an inn, feeling very excited for she has never had any money of her own to spend before. At last she comes to a small inn and enters hesitantly. Fortunately for Alice the innkeeper's wife takes to her immediately. Realising that the pretty girl is very young and inexperienced, she does not charge her more than twice the usual price for her supper and bed. Alice goes to sleep in a fairly clean bed in a nice room. She feels very grand but leaves her candle alight just in case. (After all, it is the first time she has been away from home on her own.)

In the middle of the night, something strange happens. The window catch rattles a little and then the window slowly opens and a burglar creeps in. He jumps silently down onto the floor and looks around in the dim candlelight. What's this? No luggage? Isn't this one of the best rooms? He is very disappointed. No, there is nothing except a pretty girl asleep in the bed. She does not even have a pack. There is a letter on the table. The burglar picks it up and shakes it. No money inside. However, he sees that it is addressed to Sir William of Scarborough Castle. Intrigued, he carefully peels the seal up without breaking it and reads the contents. His jaw drops.

'Dear brother, as soon as you get this letter please kill the bearer. See you next week. Yr affectionate brother, John Kt of Yrk.'

The burglar is shocked. 'What a horrible trick to play on such a pretty girl!' he thinks. 'What a bastard John Kt of Yrk must be! Hmm. I'll settle his hash for him!'

Very carefully the burglar scrapes a word from the letter with his knife and inserts a few. Smiling, he warms the seal over the bedroom candle and sticks it down again. Then, with a pleasant feeling of having down something good for a change, the burglar slips out of the window and is gone into the night.

In the morning, Alice sets out for Scarborough again and by the evening has arrived. It is a steep climb up to the castle and she is tired, but eventually she finds herself standing before the great doors. The guard on duty takes one look at the address on the letter and allows her to enter. He takes the letter from her, telling her to wait for his master. Time goes by. Alice sits on a mounting block by the gate, waiting. Suddenly there is a great bustle and a man who looks very like the Knight of York comes rushing down some stairs and, taking her by both hands gives her a kiss on the cheek. 'Welcome!' he says. 'It's a bit of a surprise, I must say. Never thought old John was such a romantic, but you are a pretty girl and I suppose he thinks it is better for his son to be happy rather than rich. Come and meet him.'

Not daring to speak, Alice is hustled upstairs to where a handsome young man is standing. He looks as confused as Alice.

'I know it's sudden, but she's much better looking than that rich old dowager he was thinking of for you, lad.'

'What?' stammers the young man. His uncle waves the letter under his nose.

'It's all here in black and white! Listen, I'll read it! "Dear brother, as soon as you get this letter please marry the bearer to my son." It couldn't be clearer and you know how angry he'll get if we don't do exactly what he says! He'll be here next week. Call the priest!'

And so, before either of them can do anything other than exchange helpless glances, Alice and the Knight of York's son, Gregor, are married to each other.

Sudden the marriage may be, but it seems to be successful. Gregor and Alice take to each other straight away and spend the first week of their marriage very happily. Alice loves not having to gut fish and Gregor is very relieved not to be married to an aged dowager.

The following Saturday as they are sitting in a window embrasure merrily cheating each other at chess they hear a great blowing of horns and the sound of many hooves. Servants start running about all over the place. It is the Knight of York.

Sir William fondly embraces his brother but is somewhat surprised when he whispers in his ear, 'Did you get my letter?'

''Course I did!' says Sir William. 'Delighted to do what you wanted!'

Sir John glances around in a worried manner. 'Ssssh!' he says. 'Keep your voice down! You did it then?'

'I did! Great idea! They seem very happy!'

'What are you babbling about?'

'Your son and Alice ...'

Up in the solar the newly-weds are alarmed to hear the sounds of a very loud angry voice coming their way. They jump to their feet just as the Knight of York bursts in with his sword drawn. Before anyone can do anything, he has seizes Alice by her long hair and drags her down the stairs, shouting for his horse. Gregor runs behind his father, begging him to put the sword down, but as soon as the knight reaches the courtyard he throws Alice over the saddle and leaps up behind her. 'No son of mine is going to wed a wretched pauper!' he cries and with that he gallops out of the castle, away down the hill with his horse's hooves striking sparks from the stones as he goes.

Alice is terrified, but she keeps begging the knight to release her as she has done nothing but what he asked. His only reply is to spur his horse even harder.

When they reach the beach, he flings her from the horse and stands over her with that great sword in his hand. Poor Alice's lip is bleeding and her hair all tangled. She kneels in the sand and, weeping, begs the knight to let her go. 'I'll go away forever!' she cries. 'I'll disappear if only you let me live.'

Despite himself the knight is moved; after all she is very pretty even in this state. He lowers his sword. 'Forever?'

'Forever! I swear it!'

Forever is just a word to her, thinks the knight. Let us make sure she knows what it means. He takes a heavy silver ring from his finger. 'This is what forever means, girl!' he says throwing the ring into the sea. 'It means that you swear not to come near me or any one of my family until the day you can show me that very ring on your hand!'

Alice swears, crying bitterly. Then, in a swirl of sand and a thud-ding of hooves, the knight is gone, leaving her to pick up the pieces of her life alone.

For a while, Alice can think of nothing. She wanders down the beach, weeping. Then, as the day wanes, she realises that she is going to have to make a plan. What is she to do? She cannot go back to her family because she has already sent them a message telling them about her marriage. She does not want them to worry about her and anyway, they live too near the knight. She has a little money left over from that gold noble, but that will not keep her for long. She will have to beg her bread to start with and hope to find work in one of the little villages north of Scarborough. Slowly she begins the long walk through the town into the country.

For many days Alice walks, begging her bread as she goes. Women usually feel sorry for her as she is so young, but she soon learns to hide from men when the sun goes down. Eventually one day she stops at a gentleman's house to beg and finds out that there is a job going there. It is only as a skivvy, but at least she will have a bed and a roof over her head.

Actually, it turns out better than she could have hoped for, because the family and servants turn out to be kind and easy-going. They like her because she is so quiet and hard-working. Soon the mistress of the house, whose name is also Alice (what did I tell you?) has come to trust her with buying food and even cooking certain meals. At the year's end her master and mistress give her a pretty new dress.

'When will a skivvy ever get to wear that?' she asks the little foot-page sadly as they sit peeling carrots. 'You never know,' he says, 'perhaps on your wedding day!' He means to cheer her up, so he is shocked to see big tears fall down her cheeks. When he asks her what the matter is, she just shakes her head.

Towards the end of spring, the house is filled with excitement because the master of the house has decided to have a great banquet to celebrate his birthday. He intends to invite all his friends from across Yorkshire. For a fortnight, the house is cleaned from top to bottom and extra servants are hired to help with the cooking. The lady of the house wants, in particular, to have a really good fish dish to impress the guests, she informs Alice. 'Now, my dear, you told us that you are the daughter of a fishmonger. Do you think you are able to choose and cook a perfect fish for us?'

Alice nods. 'I knew a special secret recipe of my mother's. I'm sure it will impress.'

Two days before the birthday, the guests begin to arrive in dribs and drabs. Alice and the other servants keep peering out of the windows to see them arrive in all their finery.

'Ooo! Look at that gorgeous horse!' sighs a maid. Alice glances out of the scullery window and there before her is the grey stallion of the Knight of York trotting into the courtyard. She freezes in terror. Surely it cannot be … Yes, there is the knight riding him! And, see! Following behind is a coal-black horse carrying her very own husband. She ducks down out of sight, her heart pounding. How was she to know that the knight was a friend of her master? What is she to do? Her first instinct is to flee, but at that very minute there is a loud banging at the kitchen door and she has to answer it. The jolly red-faced local fishmonger stands there carrying in his two arms a simply enormous fish.

'Hello love. Thought your mistress might like this for the feast tomorrow,' he says. 'It's a bargain at two shillings!'

For once it seems that the attractive kitchen maid is not going to quibble. She seems distracted and pays up immediately. He thrusts the fish into her arms and leaves before she changes her mind.

When the cook comes in Alice is still standing there. 'What are you doing with that fish? Teaching it to dance?' snaps the cook. 'Get on and clean it, you silly girl!' Slowly Alice puts it down on the table and begins mechanically to slit open its stomach and pull out its entrails. Can she hide from the knight? Can she get a secret message to her husband? Does he still love her?

She puts her hand into the cavity of the fish's stomach. That's a bit odd, she thinks. What is this hard lump? She looks at what

she has drawn out. At first she cannot see what it is, but when she has swished it in a bowl of clean water she gasps. It is a heavy silver ring; the very one the knight threw into the sea. Slowly a rare smile dawns on her pale face. Thinking hard, she places the ring on her own finger.

The banquet, when it finally happens, sounds, to those in the kitchen, to be a great success. The servants can hear the ooos and aahs of delight as each course is brought in. 'It's time to take in the fish!' says the cook. 'It looks good but I hope you haven't forgotten the salt, girl!' Alice smiles nervously and clasps her hands together as the serving man picks up the beautifully decorated dish and carries it into the hall balanced on the tips of his fingers. For a few minutes, there is silence as it is carved and distributed to the guests, and then there is a storm of clapping and delighted comments. The little foot-page runs in.

'Oh! Alice!' he shouts excitedly. 'They love it! They're demanding to see the person who cooked it!'

'Humph!' says the cook. 'Go on then, girl!'

Alice looks at her dirty hands and grubby dress. 'Stall them for a moment while I tidy myself up!' she gasps. Then she runs up to her room, changes into the new dress and quickly brushes her hair. In five minutes she is down again, shyly pushing open the door of the great hall.

As she enters all the ladies say, 'Oh! How sweet!' and all the gentlemen stroke their beards and try to look particularly manly – all except two. The Knight of York utters a terrible oath and leaps to his feet. His son also leaps to his feet but with hope in his eyes. 'You!' they both say. Then the knight vaults over the table and, drawing his sword, rushes towards Alice with a terrible look of fury on his face.

Alice does not move. Instead she holds up her hand so that he can see the silver ring shining on her hand. He stops as if he has been stabbed, and his mouth opens and shuts stupidly, rather as though he were a large fish himself. He cannot think of a single thing to say, but Gregor can. He too vaults over the table and folds his wife in his arms. 'My Alice!' he exclaims. 'My own Gregor!' she replies. 'Aaah!' say all the ladies, wiping their eyes. The men all shuffle their feet and start talking loudly about hunting.

And so it is that the son of the Knight of York does indeed stay married to a pauper called Alice Sidebottom, and in the end the knight has to accept it. (He eventually becomes quite fond of her.)

After all, he was the one silly enough to want to know the future in the first place, and who among us is clever enough to escape the fate foretold by the *Book of Fate*?

## Robin Hood and the Knight

(This tale is one of the oldest of the Robin Hood stories, and as it involves St Mary's Abbey in York I have included it here.)

'Will you not sit down to your meat, Robin?' said Will Scarlett.

'No, by Christ! Not until we have welcomed some unexpected guest. You, Much and Little John must go and wait by Watling Street. Bring me a traveller or I swear we'll all go hungry today!'

Grumbling, the three men took their bows, slung their sheaves of arrows on their backs and stomped off through the forest to the high road.

'Fancies himself King Arthur!' muttered Much the Miller's Son. 'I'm starving!'

Little John thumped him on the shoulder. 'We're outlaws, man! We have to earn our living.' They peered gloomily along the empty road.

It could not have been more than a quarter of an hour – though to hungry men it seemed longer – before the sound of approaching hooves could be heard.

'Hush!' hissed Will Scarlett. 'I think dinner's about to arrive!' The three men hid swiftly.

'Sounds like a knight's horse!' said Much. 'A very old one, though.'

Through the trees they glimpsed the traveller. He was indeed a knight, but the most miserable-looking knight you can imagine. His tired old horse shambled along with a drooping head. Its bridle was mended with rope and the stuffing was coming out of its saddle. The man who rode it was scarcely better for his head too hung low and his clothes were dirty and torn. His rusty sword showed through the holes in its sheath; his boots were scuffed and muddy. Altogether he was a picture of misery.

The outlaws looked at each other and shrugged. He was a knight and therefore he must be rich – richer than them at any rate. Little John stepped out into the knight's path, holding his bow before him with an arrow half drawn.

'Hold! Sir Knight!' he said.

'What?' The knight came out of his gloomy reverie with a jump. His horse stopped and began grazing.

'Welcome, Sir Knight. Our master Robin Hood would be very happy if you would do him the honour of dining with him.'

The knight stared blankly at the three outlaws. 'Would you mind repeating that?'

Little John repeated the invitation very slowly.

'Oh – Robin Hood – I see. Do I have any choice in the matter?'

The three escorted the knight through the woods. Soon the rich smell of cooking meat reached their nostrils. The knight began to cheer up a little. As they got closer to the camp he saw broad tables set out under huge oak trees. They were covered with snowy linen and spread with all sorts of good things. Venison there was, of course, pork too and a baron of beef, all well garnished with dishes of vegetables. There was bread and butter, cheese and honey, all of the very best. The knight's face lit up.

'Your master Robin must be a rich man,' he said. 'This is a spread fit for a king!'

As he spoke, an archer dressed in a simple Lincoln green tunic approached and bowed to him. He had lively bright blue eyes and a brown, somewhat weather-beaten, face.

'Please alight from your horse, honoured guest,' he said. 'I am Robin Hood and it is my pleasure to welcome you to my table.'

Soon the knight was sitting at his ease with a laden trencher and a goblet of good wine in his fist. He had not eaten for a long time so for a while there was little talk. Robin observed his guest as he ate. The man seemed starving. That he really was a knight was certain, but that he was down on his luck was sure too.

When the knight's hunger was a little abated, Robin asked him his name and where he came from. The knight looked up from a dish of warden pears, took another mouthful of wine and said, 'My name is Richard at the Lee and I hold lands in Wyresdale. Thank you for a most unlooked for and delicious dinner, Master Robin! If ever I can repay you, I will.'

'Ah, now. Talking of repayment. It is our custom to feast our guests well, but we also expect them to pay for what you must admit is a very generous entertainment.'

Sir Richard's face, which until that moment had looked almost cheerful, fell.

'Alas!' he said. 'I don't have any money worth talking of. Just ten shillings in my saddlebag. Go and see if you don't believe me.'

Robin nodded to Much who went to get the knight's moneybag. When he came back he tipped out its contents onto the table and everyone could see that the knight had spoken the truth.

'How do you come to be in this sad state?' asked Robin. The knight looked around at all the outlaws who were sitting expectantly, leaning with their elbows on the tables: they loved a good story.

'Good yeomen, my tale is a sad one. I have but one son; a fine young man, strong, well educated and bred to be a knight. He wished to improve our family fortunes by making a name for himself at tournaments, so, although I was not very rich I laid out money on the very best horse and armour I could afford. Unfortunately in his very first melée he had the misfortune to kill the son of a great Lancastrian lord.' The outlaws shook their heads and murmured sympathetically. They knew what it was to fall foul of the great.

'And so this lord wanted compensation?' asked Robin.

'He did indeed, far more than I could pay. What could I do? My son would languish in a Lancastrian gaol until I paid up, so I borrowed the £400 from the Abbot of St Mary's Abbey in York, thinking that he was a Christian soul who would understand my problem. However, he demanded that, as a pledge, I mortgage my lands to him, to be redeemed in a year's time. That year is up tomorrow; scrimp and save as I have I have not been able to get so much money together in such a short time. That ten shillings is all I have collected. My son is free, but he will lose his inheritance tomorrow unless I can persuade the abbot to extend the loan. Knowing the abbot as I now do, I have little hope of that. Alas! What is a knight without lands? Nothing better than a common soldier!'

Robin Hood listened carefully to the story. Then he clapped his visitor on the back. 'What do you think, friends?' he asked his outlaws. 'Shall we help this good knight?'

'Aye!' they shouted with one voice.

Robin turned to his guest. 'Sir Richard, cheer up! I shall lend you the money you need.' Sir Richard gasped; he could not believe his ears! 'That is more than generous! But how do you know I will ever be able to repay you? Must I now mortgage my lands to you?'

Robin laughed. 'What would I do with lands when I have all the forest?' he said. 'No I need no surety – or rather, let us say that Our Lady will be your surety. I have never known her to fail me. Can you repay me in another year?'

The knight nodded, dumbly.

'Then all I need is your word as a knight that you will do so.'

'It is given!'

'Good. Now, we cannot have you visiting the great Abbot of St Mary's dressed like that and riding such a sorry nag. I'll give you a better horse and clothes fit for a gentleman!'

Robin was as good as his word. By the afternoon, the knight, looking much happier than when he had arrived, was trotting down Watling Street on a fine dapple-grey horse. He was dressed in good broadcloth lined with silk and Little John ran beside him as a servant to see that all went well. The only thing the knight kept of his old clothes was his worn and patched cloak.

By that evening, they reached York and put up at the Black Swan. The next morning, hiding his fine new clothes beneath his old cloak, Sir Richard went to keep his noon appointment with the abbot.

The abbey of St Mary had become vast and wealthy over the years. Many of the monks were lazy and haughty and of all these the abbot was the worst: a huge fat man with a fur-lined gown over his monk's robe who dined like a prince every day.

On this day, he was seated next to the High Justice of England whom he had invited to witness Sir Richard's expected failure to redeem his mortgage. The two men were old cronies and, having drunk deeply, were laughing and joking at Sir Richard's expense.

'Looked like a beaten dog!' chortled the abbot. 'I knew immediately he'd never be able to pay so I didn't hesitate!'

'You're such a bad man!' giggled the high justice. 'They're very fine lands, I hear. A nice plum to fall into your hands! I hope you won't forget the service I'm doing you!'

The prior, who was dining with them, ventured to hope that Sir Richard might yet be able to pay. 'After all we know he's a good man.' The other two laughed even louder at that and the abbot was forced to wipe his eyes on a corner of the tablecloth.

Meanwhile Sir Richard was being dealt with less than politely by the abbot's servants, who knew all about his problems. Seeing his patched cloak, they at first pretended to think he was a beggar and kept him waiting for a long time before they would let him in. It was only when Little John threatened to knock their heads off that they finally opened the door.

'Sir Richard Lackland to see your lordship!' announced a smiling wag. Sir Richard slowly walked up the long refectory. The abbot leaned back in his carved chair and beckoned him forward with an insulting wave of his hand. 'Ah! Sir Richard,' he said, 'you needn't have bothered wearing your Sunday best! Have you come to pay me back my money?'

Sir Richard knelt before him with lowered head. The abbot and the high justice exchanged triumphant glances. 'My lord, I have not yet been able to amass such a large sum. I have come to beg for your well-known mercy and kindness. Please allow me another year –' He got no further.

The abbot stood up majestically and sneered at the humble, kneeling figure. 'You ungrateful wretch! I extended my generosity to you and you have failed me! I needed that money for holy works! This all comes of your indulgence to your feckless son. Now, I shall be forced to burden myself with your worthless lands. This worthy justice is here to witness your failure.' He turned to the justice. 'Have you got the documents?'

Sir Richard sprang to his feet and threw off his patched cloak. The abbot backed away in alarm, tripped and fell into his chair. The knight pulled out a bulging bag from under his belt.

'Cruel man, as greedy as you are unfeeling! You insult your holy vows!' shouted the knight. 'See!' he pulled a small round table towards him and upended the large pouch onto it. Gold poured out and spilled clinking onto the floor.

'You call yourself the servant of God but I say you are a servant of the Devil! If you had been merciful I would have paid you even more interest, but Robin Hood is my banker now!' He turned on his heel and marched from the hall, followed by the grinning Little John. The abbot and the justice stared after him like idiots. Only the prior, smiling to himself, felt like continuing the meal.

A year later, Little John, Much the Miller's Son and Will Scarlett were once again leaning against trees beside Watling Street.

'Do you think he'll turn up?' Much asked the others.

'Well, he's a knight, isn't he?' said Will. 'It's a matter of honour for him.'

'Just as well we're not knights, eh?' said Little John and they all laughed. Suddenly Will signalled for them to hide themselves. Someone was coming from the direction of York, so the outlaws knew immediately that it could not be Sir Richard. The sound was of many hooves trotting. As the travellers came into view, the outlaws set arrow to bowstring. First came a fat monk riding on a sturdy mule and leading another, well laden. Behind him were four nervous-looking men-at-arms on ponies.

Little John stepped out into their path with his arrow pointed at the monk's fat belly.

'Hold, Sir Monk!' he said politely.

The monk's face became a furious red. 'Stand aside, man. I am on important business for the Abbot of St Mary's. Stand aside or my men will run you down!'

The men-at-arms looked even more nervous if possible. They began to mutter among themselves and to back their ponies. Little John lowered his bow. 'But if I let you continue it will interfere with my own master's business!'

The men-at-arms turned their ponies around. One of them shouted, 'No offence meant – wouldn't dream of interfering with Master Robin's business. Just going!' And before the astonished monk could say a word his escort had turned tail and cantered briskly away.

'Cowards! Poltroons!' he yelled after them.

Will now stepped forward and bowed. 'Sir Monk, we would not dream of hurting a man of the cloth. All we want is for you to dine with our master today.'

What could he do? Little John already had his hand on the mule's rein so the monk had to put on the best face he could as he was led into the forest.

'I'll stay and wait for Sir Richard,' said Much. 'Save me some dinner!'

The monk could not complain about his treatment. Robin Hood was as courteous as he could wish and when he saw the greenwood feast spread out he began to think that all might be well. Soon he was gobbling as happily as if he was in his own refectory.

His tongue was loosened by an excellent claret that Robin pressed on him. Before long he had revealed that he was the cellarer of St Mary's and was on his way to London on the abbot's business, buying wine.

'So you work for Our Lady Mary?' asked Robin.

'Well, in a manner of speaking, I suppose so. The abbey does technically belong to her.'

'Excellent!' Robin exclaimed. 'What do you think, men, has this good monk been sent to pay Our Lady's debt?'

'Aye! Aye! Aye!' shouted all the outlaws, banging on the tables with their knife handles.

The monk looked confused. 'What debt? I don't know anything about any debt!'

'You see, master Monk, Our Lady Mary stood guarantor of a loan and as this is the day it must be redeemed and as the borrower isn't here, it's time for her to pay it back. She's made you her holy instrument, you fortunate man!'

The blood drained from the monk's face. 'B-but I've only got twenty marks on me. Just enough to get me to London!'

'Little John, go and see whether what he says is true. If it is then, of course, you may keep it!'

Needless to say Little John returned from the baggage mule with several small sacks that chinked satisfyingly. When they had counted all of the coins, they found that the monk had been carrying £800. The outlaws laughed and laughed at his discomfit.

'What a woman that sweet Lady Mary is!' said Robin Hood, running his fingers through the shining coins. 'I've never known a better security! She's paid her debt twice over!'

It was vain for the monk to argue and plead and even weep, swearing that it was the abbey's money needed to buy food for the poor. They put him back on his mule and sent on his way with nothing but a good dinner inside him and a few mocking bows.

Now, at last, Much came back with Sir Richard. 'He's here!' shouted Much. 'He was delayed, but he's here and he's brought the money, just as he promised!'

Robin greeted him with pleasure. 'I always knew that you would keep your word. But by God, it's a miracle! Two debtors have repaid their debts voluntarily in one day!'

Sir Richard looked surprised. 'Two?'

'Aye. And it bodes well for you, my friend. We have made £800 today from the Abbot of St Mary's. Keep your money; your debt is cancelled. And here is another £400 to gild your spurs with!'

Sir Richard was speechless at his good fortune – raising the £400 had been hard work and he and his family had had to go without during the last year.

'Cheer up, Sir Richard!' said Little John. 'You're a bit late for dinner but you're just in time for an early supper. We don't want your wife saying that we haven't fed you properly!' And so, surrounded by Robin Hood and his merry men, Sir Richard at the Lee, sat under the broad sunlit boughs of the forest oaks and ate the happiest meal of his life.


## Dick Turpin

Thank you for your kind interest, gentlemen. If only we had time, I could make a fine tale of my life, but dawn being all too close your curiosities will have to be satisfied with this sorry brief digest!

I was born in the year 1705 at Thaxtead in the county of Essex where my father was a butcher who also kept a public house. We often saw the gentry passing through. How fine they seemed to me with their grand clothes and their noses in the air! From my earliest years my ambition was to become such a gentleman, with a carriage and servants. To that end, knowing that education was needed, I went to school more willingly than many boys. What dreams we have when we are children! How soon they are dashed! It was my misfortune that my father could afford nothing better than the local common school where I learnt to write a fair hand, but

nothing more useful to the achievement of my ambition. Seeing this
– for I was always of a keen intelligence – it was not long before the
play of my schoolmates became more attractive to me than work.
I fear we led our schoolmaster, a Mr Smith, many a sad dance.

My education ceased when my father decided I should be appren-
ticed to a butcher like himself. I liked the work well enough but the
price the farmers asked for their beeves often left us with little profit.

Not long after I completed my apprenticeship I wedded Mary
Palmer of East Ham. We had no money and our parents were not
well pleased, but she said to me that we would make our fortunes
one of these days so why wait?

The acquisition of money was our main topic of conversation.
Soon we were in debt and almost starving, for the butcher I was
working for turned me off for stealing. Well, thinks I, if I already
have the name of a thief then I should at least profit by my new occu-
pation. So, I stole a bullock from a fat local farmer and butchered it
behind our cottage. Mary sold the meat in the market. It brought us
enough blunt to live on for a while and so I did it again, and again,
always being careful to pick different farmers so that none suffered
too much. My Mary called me another Robin Hood.

All went well enough until two scrubs, servants to Mr Giles of
Plaistow, peached on me to the magistrates. They had seen me
driving off two of his oxen so I had to escape from my home sharp-
ish, without my dear Mary. She proved true, however, sending me
money to get me down to the coast.

I was somewhat disheartened by this failure of mine. From
now on, I thought, I shall leave butchering and engage in a more
gentlemanly trade. With this in mind it so chanced that I fell in with
a party of men who told me of a new venture in fine wines and spirits.
'We sell only to rich men and connoisseurs!' they said, thinking me,
as I supposed, no more than a rum cully, but I, not being as green
as they thought, took to the smuggling trade (for that was in fact
their venture) so well that they soon looked to me as a leader.

All went well until the Excise grew so hot upon us that we had to
remove to Epping Forest where we lived very hand-to-mouth, stealing in a small way. Then one day one of my associates returned from

attempting to rob a little farm. He brought us a new idea. He had been driven off with blows and insults and he now thought that if we went in a body we would meet little resistance. 'That old tit would have sung another tune if you had all been there to help me!'

So it was that we hit upon our greatest plan: we would work all the lonely farms around the forest as a gang, and see what a little persuasion would squeeze out. Soon we became quite famous: the Essex Gang, we were called. It was easy work, especially on market day when the men of the farm were in town. The servants gave us little trouble and soon yellowboys and jewels flowed into our pockets. We were in clover!

You will hear people say that we were torturers, but that is a black lie. A few slaps, a twisted arm soon made the woman of the house – what shall we say – keen to accommodate us with the keys to her strongbox. It was only with those who attacked us that we were severe.

It was a sweet enough lay for a while. We had enough to live like kings in the taverns around the forest at all of which we were welcome. However, as our fame grew it came to the notice of the king himself. He offered £50 for the apprehension of me and my gang. No one in Essex dared attempt it though, we made sure of that.

The day my luck turned we had just done the sweetest job: old man called Francis, in Marylebone. We had tied up his servants and beaten his wife and daughter – for the old fool wouldn't tell us where his valuables were. In the end he gave us a fine haul: gold, some of it; there was a watch, I remember, and some rings as well as other stuff. Unfortunately he was fly enough to get the Bow Street Runners onto us afterwards. I only just got away, but they got two of my boys, damn their eyes, and hanged them without mercy.

After that I went solo for a while. It's amazing how far a polite address and a good suit of clothes will take you, for no one distrusts a gentleman – though in my experience, they are snakes, every one. My biggest need was more blunt – for some better duds to improve my appearance.

At that time highwaymen were all the rage. There were ballads and chapbooks about them everywhere. Gay's *The Threepenny Opera* had come out not long before and everyone, including me, fancied himself MacHeath.

Well, thought I, I want to be a gentleman and highwaymen are gentlemen of the road, so why delay further? I betook myself with my pistols to the Cambridge Road and waited for my prey.

Soon a well-dressed man came riding along. I stood forth into his path with my pistols pointed at his breast saying 'Stand and deliver!' To my surprise he merely laughed.

'Well said, my lad. Almost like a highwayman! What's your name?'

'Dick Turpin!' says I.

'Well, Dick my cully, I've heard of you,' says he, 'and I fancy you've heard of me, for I am Captain Tom King!'

That is how I joined forces with the most famous highwayman of his day. He took a liking to me and we agreed to share our ventures and to lodge together in a secret cave between King's Oak and Loughton Road. We worked the roads through Epping Forest. Do not think that we were at all ill-housed in a cave, for everything we needed was supplied by my dear Mary, who had been living at this time on the earnings of a little public house I had procured for her when I was a smuggler. She brought us food and drink; many a merry party did we have together.

My acquaintance with Captain Tom did much to improve my manner, for he was a gentleman born and bred. He taught me much, laughing often at my ignorance and country ways. I brooked his correction knowing that it would help me in the future, as indeed it did.

The fickle wheel of fortune turned once more when a foolish man called Morris, inspired with greed for the £100 at which my bounty now stood, came after me. I was forced to shoot him and though it was in self-defence and entirely his own fault, in the eyes of the law I was now a murderer The bounty on my head was raised to £200 and a description of me printed and spread abroad. It was not flattering, but it was near enough to cause me trouble:

> About five foot nine inches high, very much marked with the smallpox, his cheeks broad, his face thinner towards the bottom, his visage short, pretty upright and broad about the shoulders.

Tom King was not pleased with me. We quarrelled about Morris, but we went on working together. Then one night he went to Whitechapel to pick up a good horse that I had conned out of a man called Major. The Runners were waiting there, thinking to get both of us and claim the reward. You will hear scrubs bad-mouthing me but I never meant to shoot Tom; I was aiming at the Runners. My horse tossed his head as I shot and the ball went wide and hit Tom instead. He fell like a dead man. I overcame my horror enough to escape but later I heard that poor Tom lingered on for a week before he died. Better than hanging? No, it was no way for a highwayman to go.

After that I had to get out of Essex. The last time I saw my Mary, for she died soon after, she begged me to go north, saying that she had no wish to see me dance on empty air at the gallows. She gave me some money and food and I left my old haunts forever.

This time I set myself up in Lincolnshire at a place called Long Sutton. The fame of Dick Turpin being less well known here, I rented an apartment and dressed as a gentleman, being accepted as such by my neighbours.

You may think that my life would now be peaceful but the truth is that I was soon tired of this quiet life. There were no easy chubs to cheat at cards and no light women to drink with. After a time, some of my old acquaintances came into the county and I fell into my former ways. There were plenty of very fine horses around, not well guarded and so we turned to 'prigging gallopers' as my vulgar friends called it.

It was a good trade for I could easily sell the disguised horses in York. I soon gained a great acquaintanceship there where I passed as a wealthy horse trader. I called myself Palmer, after my dear Mary. After a time I decided to remove there, York being a fine city and much more to my taste than Lincolnshire.

One evening, I was riding home with some of my rich friends when my landlord's cockerel came strutting out in front of us, crowing fit to burst your ears. On a whim, I shot it, occasioning much mirth in my companions as well as praise for my shooting. My landlord was not so happy though and the rogue clapped a fastener on me. I had to appear before the magistrates in Beverley and was remanded on bail. This was my downfall, for I had no ready money on me to pay it.

The magistrate stretched his eyes and said, 'Mr Palmer, you have the appearance of a gentlemen and so I am amazed that you cannot easily pay your bail. I fear that as you are newly come to the county I must investigate you further for we want no bankrupts here nor wanted men.'

I was transferred to the debtor's prison in York Castle. Hearing that I was in trouble for money, all my creditors began to dun me. Soon questions began to be asked about the horses I had sold and I was indicted for horse stealing.

One of my prison colleagues suggested that I should get a friend from my past to write a letter of good character for me. 'This is not London,' he said, 'The magistrates here will believe what they read if it be well written.'

I thanked him and wrote to my brother, the only person I knew in the world who might be persuaded to give me a good character, for most of my old acquaintances were either dead, in prison or unable to write. I thought of Captain Tom with regret. Here is what I wrote:

Dear Brother,

I am sorry to acquaint you that I am now under confinement in
York Castle for horse stealing. If I could procure an evidence from
London to give me a character, that would go a great way towards
my being acquitted. I have not been long in this country before
being apprehended, so that it would pass off the readier.

For heaven's sake dear brother do not neglect me. You will know
what I mean when I say I am yours,

John Palmer.

Now was fortune determined to ruin me. Retribution waited to dash
me to the ground. My dear brother refused to pay the postage owed
on my letter and it was returned to the post office. By the veriest
chance, a man spotted it and thought he recognised the handwrit-
ing. He asked one of the magistrates to be allowed to open it for
he thought it was writ by the notorious highwaymen Dick Turpin.
His request was granted and so the one man who could recognise
my writing, my old teacher Mr Smith, revealed my true identity!

Now all York rejoiced that such a famous figure had been
captured in their own city. My trial was short, considering the evidence against me, but the courtroom was filled by the very best
sort of people, tender-hearted ladies weeping at my cruel fate and
men offering me drink. The court ushers roared themselves hoarse
and the judge, putting on the black cap, could scarce make himself
heard as he delivered the deadly verdict.

Since being placed in the condemned cell, which is a large room
they have here in York Gaol, I have had no peace. So many visitors
have come and gone, wringing my hand or begging a remembrance
of me. I am determined to be turned off in style; I feel I owe it to Tom
to die like a gentleman and it is in my mind to give them all a surprise.
I have ordered a new suit and shoes and distributed to my friends
what possessions remain to me. I have ordered my last meal and laid
out ten shillings for five mourners to follow the hangman's cart.

The chaplain has been here wearying me with talk of repentance but I have sent him away with a flea in his ear. Life has been good and I regret none of it except perhaps Captain Tom. Let God watch out! I mean to drink with the Devil tomorrow night. Then we'll raise Hell together!

Farewell!

Turpin was hanged at Tyburn on the Knavesmire in York on 19 April 1739. A great crowd collected to accompany the cart from the prison. Turpin bowed to them all and continued to greet acquaintances all the way to the gallows. Once there, he leapt easily up the ladder onto the scaffold. He refused a blindfold and stood with the noose around his neck, chatting to the guards and hangmen for half an hour before jumping off without assistance. He was dead in moments.

His body had some adventures of its own. It was first taken to the Blue Boar public house in Castlegate where the landlord put it in his parlour and charged visitors to see it. In the end, Dick's friends had to steal it to stop people from cutting off parts of it. (Whether for keepsakes or black magic is not clear.)

Even after burial the body did not rest in peace but was dug up several times by bodysnatchers. On one occasion it was found in the garden of a surgeon.

In the end it was buried in quicklime in the churchyard of St George's church where the grave may still be seen.

## The Pirate Archbishop

Sometimes a person appears in the world with more than usual vitality or charisma around whom folk tales begin to gather like barnacles around an old boat; Mrs Thatcher is an example from our own time.

Archbishop Blackburne of York is forgotten now, but in his day his obscure history and his less than virtuous character meant that by his death he had become, quite literally, legendary. Some of what follows may be true, but which bits?

Over the south door of York Minster there is a series of canopied arches in the centre of which, not too long ago, the statue of a fiddler once stood. It was put there by Archbishop Lancelot Blackburne to celebrate a stolen fiddle.

Lancelot was born in the middle of the seventeenth century and grew up in the wild and wicked times of the Merry Monarch, Charles II. As a second son, he was destined for the Church and was sent to Cambridge to study theology.

Life as a student in those days was – believe it or not – rather more exuberant and violent than it is now. Betting, drinking matches, horseracing, duelling, fighting, rioting and general laddishness were the pleasant pastimes of many of the richer students, despite their all

being intended for holy orders. Lancelot took to this delightful life with gusto; he played the fiddle well and was a popular addition to many a raucous party. So enthusiastically did he embrace the riotous life that, before his first term was over, he found himself 'gated' (forced to be in by 7 p.m.) for missing church.

Such a restriction was to Lancelot like a red rag to a bull. Already unhappy with the boredom of the university's teaching he decided that he did not want to stay at Oxford any more. What use was education when there was a world to explore? One afternoon he walked out of his rooms intending to run away to London. He had already exhausted the allowance from his parents and was just considering how he would earn his bread when he passed his tutor's open door. There on the table was a fine violin. Lancelot's own fiddle was a poor cheap thing, fit only to play at drunken parties, but this was a different instrument altogether. It seemed to reach out to him begging to be taken. So he took it, hiding it in the voluminous folds of his cloak. It was this superior violin that provided him with his meal ticket every night, as he busked in inns on his journey to the metropolis.

London in those days was many times smaller than it is now, but it was still large and bustling enough to daunt anyone arriving for the first time. Luckily for Lancelot he had been born and bred there, so he already knew many of its ways and secrets. Instead of going home to face the wrath of his father he survived by staying with friends and hanging around on the fringes of the court. There he managed to pick up small (usually shady) jobs from court officials. It was hard to make enough to live on though, and when he nearly died from the cold, he realised that he would have to do something more positive. He had always fancied going to sea, though he did not want to join the Navy, and so he got himself bound as an apprentice on a Newcastle collier, *Fair Sally*.

It was not really a very good way to see the world as the collier just went up and down the east coast between London and Newcastle, but then one day something happened that changed his life. *Fair Sally* was captured by the privateer schooner *Mack Broom*. Its captain was no less a person than the Irish pirate, Redmond of the Red Hand, dreaded throughout at least several of the Seven Seas.

Seeing in Lancelot a likely lad, Redmond persuaded him to join his crew and soon Lancelot was indeed seeing the world. Among other places, they visited the West Indies, newly developed for growing sugar cane, and coasted along its shores looking for rich French or Dutch ships to rob. They had a successful cruise and returned for a while to England where Lancelot, well dressed and wealthy now, swaggered around all his old haunts spending money.

One day one of his court connections told him that the king would like to see him. Filled with curiosity he was brought into the royal presence. Years first of poverty and then of debauchery were beginning to tell on Charles by this time. His eyes were pouchy and bloodshot and his moustache obviously dyed. He was keen, however, to hear about Lancelot's exploits. 'Should have turned privateer myself,' he said. 'What things you must see! West Indies, eh? Tell me, is it true what they say about the women there …?' But he was also interested in what Lancelot could tell him about the activities of the Dutch, with whom England was sporadically at war, for Charles was a shrewd ruler, despite his relaxed manner. He knew how to recognise and make use of clever people. Soon he had enlisted the young buccaneer as one of his spies to send him occasional reports of the activities of the Dutch and the French, who were becoming distressingly powerful.

Lancelot returned to the sea and in a few years was captain of his own privateer, *Black Broom*, sweeping the seas from Cyprus to Cape Wrath in fine style and amassing a comfortable fortune.

Being a pirate was a risky business, as Lancelot knew at first hand. Too many of his friends eventually ended up hanging in Execution Dock, while three tides flowed over them. He decided to retire early and enjoy his wealth in peace, so he changed his surname from Muggins to Blackburne (in memory of his ship), bought himself a gentleman's estate and settled down with a wife.

For an active man like Lancelot the charms of rural life were soon exhausted. He was still young and ambitious. Why could he not still achieve something in a more important sphere of life? The choice of employment for a gentleman was not wide in those days: politics was a dubious and expensive business; the army too dangerous; all that remained for a gentleman was the Church.

Lancelot's decision was already made for him. He would take up his old studies and become ordained.

Having friends in high places is always a help in one's career – especially at the end of the seventeenth century when influence or bribery was really the only way to get on. Lancelot employed both and soon the newly ordained churchman was shooting up the professional ladder.

We are used to the idea of churchmen being badly paid. This was not so in the past when everyone had to pay tithes (a tenth of their income) to the Church. The local vicar was usually one of the richest men in a village. Being ordained provided as good an opportunity of getting rich as any other option.

Rulers come and go. Charles died and was succeeded by his niece Mary and her husband, and then by her sister Anne. Lancelot managed to avoid being involved in the various political troubles of the times and maintained his connection with royalty. When Queen Anne died, he was made personal chaplain to George I. He got on well with the new German king, entertaining him with anecdotes and the sort of jokes his pirate friends had enjoyed. Though a new ages of politeness was about to dawn, Lancelot continued to talk with Restoration frankness. He once congratulated the new queen on being a sensible enough woman not to object to the king's mistress. Indeed, it is said that he had even officiated at a secret (and bigamous) marriage between that very mistress and the king!

Honours continued to roll in. He was made Bishop of Exeter and then Archbishop of York. The only higher position in the Church hierarchy was Archbishop of Canterbury, but Lancelot seems to have been contented with York. The fine Bishop's Palace at Bishopthorpe was now his and he could relax and smoke and drink and gamble to his heart's content with very little to worry him.

First, however, he had an old debt to repay. Through all of his troubles and successes the violin that he had stolen from his tutor had accompanied him. He had played it for rich and poor, for pirates and prelates. Now was the time to return it to its owner, Revd Lawrence Leatherhead. He did not send it on its own; it arrived encased in a costly and beautifully made case that also contained a paper appointing Revd Leatherhead to the lucrative archdeaconry of Holderness. Lancelot celebrated his own elevation to the archbishopric by ordering a statue of himself holding the violin and having it placed above the south door of York Minster.

Though he was now an archbishop, any development of holiness was not apparent. Indeed, in Brewer's *Rogues, Villains and Eccentrics* his behaviour is described as 'seldom of a standard to be expected of an archbishop'.

It was Sunday in St Mary's church in Nottingham. Lancelot had just finished confirming some new young members of the church. He turned to the local vicar who had been helping him officiate and exclaimed, 'Thank God that's over, go and get me a pipe and some tobacco – and where's the ale?'

The astonished youngsters were now treated to the improving sight of their archbishop being beaten out of the church by their own vicar with shouts of outraged respectability.

Lancelot was unperturbed – he hated vicars anyway and refused to ordain any in his last ten years. He continued to be a terrible, but apparently beloved, archbishop for the next thirty years. 'He gained more hearts than souls!' it was said. He lived openly with his mistress as well as his wife and his illegitimate son. In York, it was even said that Dick Turpin was, for a while, his butler.

Archbishop Lancelot Blackburne died at the ripe old age of eighty-four, disgracefully unrepentant to the end. He was the last of a breed of hard-drinking worldly churchmen and a legend in his own lifetime. His fiddler statue was eventually removed as 'unsuitable' for a minster, but rumour has it that affectionate fans placed it in the undercroft. I have not looked, but perhaps (if it really exists) you will find it there …

I do not want to ruin the income of those who make their living from York's famous Ghost Walks, but the following are two particularly good stories you might hear if you went on one. They are brief but unlike many told in the past, they have enough of the ring of truth about them to be believed even by today's sceptical folk.

## THE TREASURER'S HOUSE GHOSTS

Harry Martindale was eighteen in 1953, working as an apprentice plumber. One day he was told to go to the Treasurer's House near York Minster to do some work on the central heating. This house was originally the home of the minster's treasurers but it had been a private house since the last treasurer, William Cliffe, lost his post (and the treasure) at the Dissolution of the Monasteries in 1546. The building had been extensively and elegantly remodelled in the seventeenth century by subsequent owners, but heating was never a high priority, and although its last owner handed it over to the National Trust in 1930, there was little money during the Second World War to update it.

Harry had been told to do some work in one of the cellars, which was about eighteen feet square with an arched ceiling and a ramp on one side. There was a sort of trench about eighteen inches deep in the centre and what Harry did not know then was that this was an archaeological excavation revealing the Roman road that lay below the floor.

Because he had to knock a hole through the ceiling for some pipework, Harry asked the curator if he could borrow a ladder and was grudgingly given an old rickety one with several rungs missing. He started work on the ceiling at the edge of the wall.

Just before lunchtime he heard what sounded like music – no, not music, rather one long note like a trumpet. This seemed strange because the cellar was a long way from anywhere music might be being played. The noise grew louder and louder, and suddenly he realised that it was coming from the wall on which the ladder was leaning. He was standing on the third rung and a movement below him made him glance down; there, just in line with his waist on the right-hand side he saw the top of a helmet come out of the wall.

In alarm Harry stepped back and fell from the ladder, landing heavily on his behind. Uninjured but terrified he scrambled into the corner of the cellar. Whatever it was that had come out of the wall was between him and the door!

It was a Roman soldier. He was clearly visible down to the knees, but it was only when he reached the excavation trench that the rest of his legs and his sandals came into view. He walked across the cellar at a slight angle to Harry. As his body cleared the wall, he was followed, even more alarmingly, by a large horse and rider.

'Now I could see them exactly as I can see you now. They weren't no wisp of smoke, they weren't whirly, you know, the atmosphere didn't change, they were human beings as came out of the wall except they were dressed as Roman soldiers. Because I could see that, I thought all they had to do was just look to where I was and I'd had it. This is fear, I mean, fear, it's dreadful. I never went through as much fear in the police force in fifty years as what I did in that cellar.' (Harry's actual words.)

Later, it struck Harry how small these men were but at the time he could only stare in frozen amazement. They all wore leather on top – perhaps leather shirts – and what he described as 'a green material skirt with strips of leather going round'. Their helmets fastened under the chin and they had beards. On the right side they wore short swords 'like an oversized dagger' and one of them carried a large shield with a round boss in the middle (later recognised as an Anglian shield).

As they crossed the cellar and disappeared through the opposite wall, Harry could hear their movements and the sound of the horse. There was mumbling but no speech that he could distinguish. Greatly to his relief not one of them looked in his direction.

'I don't know what I would have done if they had've done!' he said later.

When the last one had gone through and he could not hear or see anything else, Harry made his escape out of the cellar. He sat shakily on the steps for some time before the old curator came along. The moment he saw Harry he said, 'By the look of you, you've seen the Roman soldiers!'

When Harry finally told his tale, better-educated folk sneered. 'Everyone knows that Roman soldiers had rectangular shields!

Why were they not wearing loricas? Where were their sarcinas?'
Harry quickly learnt to keep his mouth shut.

Then in the 1980s more began to be known about Roman soldiers of the later Empire. It seems that when the Empire began
to decline and it became more difficult to get enough soldiers to
protect its huge borders, small more-lightly armed bands of local
men were organised. There were no longer the numbers to deploy
the traditional Roman shield successfully. These British remnants of
the once mighty Empire had round shields and lived off the land.
Suddenly it seemed possible that what Harry had seen was one of
these war bands – perhaps from the time after the withdrawal of
official Roman troops – returning from some skirmish.

## THE DEATH PACT

In the early years of our glorious Queen Victoria's reign, I was on
a visit to York Minster. I was accompanied by a numerous party,
amongst whom were a gentleman and his two daughters. I was with
the eldest of these ladies, exploring the curiosities of the building at
some distance from the rest of our companions, when, on turning
from the monument to which our attention had been directed,
we observed an officer in a naval uniform advancing towards us.
It was rather an unusual circumstance to encounter a person dressed
thus in a place so far distant from the sea. I was on the point of
making some trivial observation on the subject to my companion,
when, turning my eyes towards her I saw a deathly pallor spread
over her face. Surely some powerful and contending emotions had
suddenly been excited by the presence of the stranger.

As the officer drew nearer, and his figure and features gradually
became more distinctly visible through the evening gloom and the
dim religious light of the cathedral, the lady's distress increased: she
leant heavily upon my arm appearing painfully afflicted. Shocked
at the change I had witnessed, but wholly ignorant of the cause and

supposing her to be suffering from some violent and sudden indisposition, I called to entreat the assistance of her sister. The figure in the naval uniform was now immediately before us, and the eyes of the lady fixed upon him with a gaze of silent surprise and a painful intensity of feeling. Her half-opened lips were colourless and she drew her breath heavily as though from a full and overburdened heart. The form was close upon us (it approached her side), then it paused but for an instant. As quick as thought, a low and scarcely audible voice whispered in her ear, 'There is a future state,' and the figure moved onward, towards the door of the minster.

The father of the lady arrived to help his daughter, and I, consigning her to his protection, hastened in pursuit of the mysterious visitor. No sound of retreating footsteps was to be heard on the echoing pavements of the cathedral and though I quickly left the building and searched on every side, no man in naval uniform was to be seen among flocks of the summer visitors who thronged the streets.

Baffled in my attempt find the mysterious cause of such distress, I returned in some concern to my friends. The lady was weeping on the shoulder of her father but she avoided every inquiry about the nature of her illness.

'It was slight; it was transient; it would immediately be over.' She entreated the party to continue their examination of the building, and to leave her again in my protection. The request was granted. No sooner had she thus possessed herself of an opportunity to speak in private than she implored me, with a quick and agitated voice, to conceal for a little while the occurrence of which I had been a witness. 'We shall never be believed. Besides, it is only right that my poor dear father should gradually be prepared for the misery that he is destined to undergo. I have seen the spirit, and I have heard the voice of a brother, who exists no longer; he has perished at sea. We had agreed that the one who died the first should reappear to the survivor, if it were possible, to clear up or to confirm the religious doubts which existed in both our minds.'

In due time her fears were realised: the brother was indeed no more. His death had happened on the very day and hour in which his form was seen by his sister and myself, in the north aisle of York Minster.

# NOTES

## Something to His Advantage

The story exists in several versions, he most famous being the Pedlar of Swaffham. Similar legends can be found throughout Europe and the Middle East. The earliest version is one of the poems of the *Mathanawi* titled 'In Baghdad, Dreaming of Cairo: In Cairo, Dreaming of Baghdad', by thirteenth-century Persian poet Jalal al-Din Rumi. This poem was turned into a story in the tale from *The One Thousand and One Nights: The man who became rich through a dream*.

The provenance of the writing on the pot varies; in some versions it is an old gypsy who translates gypsy writing, in others a Quaker.

## The White Doe

I struggled with this story. Its only folk tale element is the white doe which appears at the church. It was Wordsworth who linked the doe's appearance with Emily Norton in his romantic ballad 'The White Doe of Rylstone'. Local people seem to have had all sorts of rival ghostly candidates!

Victorian invention or not, the story, with its merry inattention to dates, is now an accepted North Yorkshire tale, which is why I've included it. It also gave me the chance to tell a little of the story of the Pilgrimage of Grace, an event that was extremely important across Yorkshire but, like the much earlier Harrying of the North, little known.

I must admit to playing about with the history a little. The Pilgrimage of Grace took place in 1536, but the Rising of the North, after which

Richard Norton and his eldest son were executed, was not until 1569, thirty years later. The white dear would have been very elderly by then.

A couple of the sons really did go abroad, ending up in America.

### Potter Thompson

There are many stories of the man who stumbles into King Arthur's Cave (located in various places around the country). Should the day ever come when we require that king's services it will be interesting to see where he emerges …

### The Drummer Boy

The theme of the mysterious disappearance of someone who has set off underground playing a musical instrument of some sort is fairly common. Folk music people will know the song 'Fiddler's Hill' with its 'dark way, the deep way, the way beneath the ground'.

The Gold Hole tower's supposed treasure is a misunderstanding of a medieval joke: it was the tower where all the toilets were.

The tale of a secret tunnel between monasteries, big houses and churches is to be found in every county (and, as I can attest, is one of the banes of parents' lives!). In Sheffield, one is supposed to have been found as recently as the 1960s. What no one can ever explain is *why* anyone would want to go to the bother …

### Lame Haverah

Alas, history does not bear out this story! The park, which is just outside Harrogate and well worth a visit, did and does indeed belong to the Duchy of Lancaster. There is a John O'Gaunt's tower there, but the name Haverah is thought to come not from a personal name but from the old words for Roe (deer) Hedge. The park was once a royal chase used sometimes for deer and sometimes for raising horses for the king. More recently it was used as the site for air shower arrays, tracking cosmic rays.

### Robin Hood and the Curtal Friar

I do not know why Friar Tuck was at Fountains Abbey, which was not a friary but a monastery. Friars belonged to begging orders.

Unlike monks, who were supposed to stay for life in one particular monastery, friars worked among lay people and were supported by the community. The country was divided into areas called provinces, to one of which each friar was attached. There were various friary houses in their province where they could stay, but travelling, begging and preaching were supposedly their main occupations. Friar Tuck could thus join up with Robin's band from time to time while still theoretically doing his friarly duty.

The good friar does not appear in the very earliest recorded tales of Robin Hood. The ballad of this particular story is found in the seventeenth-century manuscript called the *Percy Folio* and is dated to the mid-fifteenth century, but his prior existence is known from a dramatic fragment from the beginning of the fifteenth century. He later became a popular figure in the May Games (the only place where Maid Marion appears).

In the original ballad, he and Robin fight with swords but I have given them quarterstaves, not just because those in holy orders were forbidden edged weapons, but also because they seem rather more suitable to the combatants' stations. (J.C. Holt's *Robin Hood* offers further debate.)

### The Giant of Dalton Mill

A Yorkshire reworking of the Ulysses story.

### Wade and His Wife Bell

The story of Wade's Causeway confuses two – or maybe three – people: the demi-god Wade, the historical Wada and, just possibly, General Wade, the great eighteenth-century road builder.

The obscure Germanic god Wade was much better known in the Middle Ages than he is now. Chaucer refers to him twice but as no one wrote down the popular stories in which Wade appeared, we do not know what they were. We know that he was connected with the sea and was the father of the more famous Weyland Smith, but little more. His presence in Yorkshire probably is due to the Scandinavian influence there, but any road-building credentials are missing.

The historical Wada was an ealdorman involved in the murder of King Aethelred of Northumbria in 794. He seems to have been remembered as a local hero who may actually have lived at Mulgrave.

General Wade (1673–1748) was a soldier and a road builder. He was connected with the subduing of the Highlands. As chief of the army in North Britain (as Scotland was renamed after the Act of Union) he built 240 miles of military roads.

> If you had seen this road before it was made
> You would lift up your hands and bless General Wade.

His fame as a road-builder was very widespread and I believe it is possible that it filtered through to Yorkshire folk (who had no cause to love the Scots), becoming entangled with and enhancing their own local story.

The road is, of course, Roman. Probably built to join the Roman camp at Malton with Whitby. It is one of the best preserved examples in the country.

## The Devil's Arrows

Retold somewhere in nearly every book on Yorkshire! I'm afraid I do not know the origin of the story; there is a very different one in Robert Mortimer's *The Great Monoliths of Boroughbridge* (London: 'The Geologist', 1860).

## The Giant of Penhill

The best-known version of this story is found in R. and J. Fairfax-Blakeborough's *Grandfather's Tales*. In the original, the old man who appears to help the people is a hermit, but this did not ring true to me, which is why I have taken one possible origin of Wensleydale's name – Woden's Wood Dale – literally and turned him into the Scandinavian version, Odin. His ravens were already there in the story as well as his fellow god Thor. There are plenty of Norse connections in the Dales (the very word 'dale' is Norse), so it is not too farfetched, though the animals connected with Thor were goats, not pigs, which were sacred to the god Freyr.

Those keen on earth mysteries may be interested in the following. Ian Taylor's *The Giant of Penhill* (Northern Lights, 1987) believes that the slopes of Penhill reveal an ancient hill figure, forgotten in all but local folklore. There is a Neolithic burial mound at the top of Pen Hill and many named springs around it, making it, possibly, an ancient ritual place. There may also be a connection with nearby West Witton and its 'Burning of the Bartle' ceremony. I couldn't possibly comment.

## Loschy Hill Dragon

All Saints Nunnington does indeed have an effigy of a knight, though the animal at his feet is a stylised lion, not a dog. The knight is actually not Peter Loschy, but Sir Walter de Teyes, Lord of Stonegrave Manor. He was buried in the church in 1325.

The dragon's ability to renew itself is a theme that probably comes from Greek mythology where the Titan Alcyoneus cannot be killed as long as he falls on the earth of his own land. Athene tells Heracles to take him to another land where he cannot be renewed and so he is killed.

## The Barguest

William Hone (1780–1842) was a rather rackety writer and political journalist who was a friend of many of the great radical figures of his day. He survived numerous failed financial ventures – and debtors' prison – caused as much by his outspoken political views as by bad management. One of his numerous literary creations was *The Table Book*, a collection of odds and ends, factual, poetic and descriptive from which two of the most famous Dales' stories come; The Barguest of Trollers' Gill and the Wise Woman of Littondale. There is another barguest story in the book, apparently told by a man who had seen the creature with his own eyes. It only ran away when it saw his wife!

The barguest is one of the types of death dog found across the country.

## The Felon Sow

Rokeby is now just over the border in County Durham, but it was part of Yorkshire for centuries so I think the story belongs here.

The poem first appears in print in Whitaker's *History of Craven*, but it was written in the fifteenth century, possibly in Richmond. Its mock-heroic style pokes fun at friars, common butts for humour at the time. 'Felon' here means 'evil'.

## The Gytrash

Goathland, near Whitby, is probably the most visited place on the North York Moors, partly because of the steam railway nearby, partly because of the TV series 'Heartbeat', which was filmed there. Tourists visiting the Mallyon Spout waterfall or avoiding the aggressive sheep (which will get into your car uninvited if there's a sandwich to be had) have no idea of the dark story connected with the village,

Gytrashes are usually dogs, or occasionally horses. They are mentioned by Charlotte Bronte in *Jane Eyre*:

> As this horse approached, and as I watched for it to appear through the dusk, I remembered certain of Bessie's tales, wherein figured a North-of-England spirit called a 'Gytrash,' which, in the form of horse, mule, or large dog, haunted solitary ways, and sometimes came upon belated travellers, as this horse was now coming upon me.

Why this one happens to be a goat is unexplained; it may be because the name Goathland was popularly thought to have something to do with goats.

## Hobs

Richard Blakeborough's *Wit, Character, Folklore and Customs of the North Riding of Yorkshire* contains much more information on different hobs in the area. They were very widely believed in. The Farndale hob story is the most commonly told and variants appear in different districts. Hob also appears in many names: Hob Cross, Hob Green, Hob Moor etc. They seem to have got everywhere!

Occasionally instead of being helpful hobs took on the character of boggarts, haunting roads to frighten people and being general nuisances.

## Elbolton Hill

It is one of the mysteries of folklore that fairies appear to prefer prehistoric sites. Whether that is because of some sort of folk memory, or whether the places themselves have a numinous quality that humans respond to is debateable. At any rate, the Elbolton fairies could not have chosen a more ancient place, because in the late nineteenth century an excavation in the oddly named Navvy Noodle Hole found the remains of eleven burials and one cremation. Pottery found with them was dated to the late Neolithic and early Bronze Age (3,000–2,000 BC). The whole area has many stones, tumuli, circles etc., from that period. Beneath the burials were older layers containing bones from cold-weather animals: reindeer, arctic fox, mountain hare, ptarmigan and bear.

For non-gardeners: fairy rings are rings of darker grass that appear in lawns and which were considered to be caused by the dancing of fairies. (I have one in my own garden.) They are in fact caused by many different types of toadstool and can be dated by their size. According to Wikipedia, one of the largest rings ever found is in France. It is about 600 metres (2,000 feet) in diameter and over 700 years old.

## The White Birds

This story comes from H.I. Gee's *Folk Tales of Yorkshire*.

## The Loaf of Bread

From Parkinsons *Folk tales of Yorkshire, Vol 1*.

## Semer Water

There are many versions of this popular tale. In some, the beggar is a holy hermit but the result is always the same. Classically minded readers may recall the selfish city turned into a lake by Zeus and Mercury, only in that case the aged couple with whom they have stayed persuade the gods to restore it.

The evil city turned into a lake and the inhabitants becoming fish also appears in *The Thousand and One Nights*.

### The Devil's Bridge

The story is mentioned in Marie Hartley & Ella Pontefract *Wharfedale* (Skipton: Dalesman Publishing Co. Ltd November, 1988).

### The Wise Woman

Another story from William Hone's *Table Book* (London: Thomas Tegg, 1841). I have used the original words mostly, only leaving out a few rhetorical flourishes (and Latin quotes).

Hone tells the story according to the literary conventions of his day. He begins by saying he was talking to another traveller in a Craven pub when the subject of the local belief in witchcraft arose. Hone, the eighteenth-century sceptic, does not believe in it, but his companion says that, being a local, he had had personal experience of it. The Wise Woman of Littondale is the story he tells.

### Old Nanny

This version is from *Folk Tales of Yorkshire* by H.L. Gee (London: Thomas Nelson & Sons, 1952), but it is widely told.

### Nine of Hearts

This story and the one that follows it comes from *Wit, Character, Folklore and Customs of the North Riding of Yorkshire* by Richard Blakeborough (London: H. Frowde, 1898). He seems to have had it almost verbatim from local people whose grandparents remembered Molly Cass. She died in the middle of the eighteenth century.

Why the nine of hearts coming up nine times should result in Old Nick having your soul, I do not know. Nine (3x3) is magic, of course, but not usually evil (unlike '666'). In cartomancy (divination by cards) the nine of hearts is called the Wish Card.

### Mother Shipton

All sorts of information is available about Mother Shipton. She almost certainly did not exist, but her prophesies live on – at least in cyberspace.

Further reading might include: Richard Head's *The Strange and Wonderful History of Mother Shipton*, (London: Richard Lownds, 1686);

*The Life and Prophecies of Ursula Sontheil: Better Known as Mother Shipton* by J.C. Simpson (Knaresborough: Dropping Well booklet); or *Mother Shipton: Her Legendary Life*, Daniel Parkinson's online article from the Mysterious Britain site.

## Ragnar Lodbrok

This story comes from *The Saga of Ragnar Lodbrok* translated by Ben Waggoner (New Haven, USA: Troth Publications, April 2009); it was written about AD 1400. Ragnar himself as an historical figure is very evasive, he, too, may not have existed at all, although other people in his story including King Aelle and Ivar the Boneless certainly did. It is possible that Ragnar is the same person as the Reginhari who sacked Paris in AD 845.

The saga includes other exciting deeds of Ragnar and his sons. It incorporates themes from folk tales from all over Europe; his shaggy breeches come from Russia for example and the snake pit probably comes from a similar story in the Völsunga Saga. I have tried to give a flavour of the terse style of the sagas, though leaving out or simplifying the obscure verses Ragnar chants.

Ivar may have been called Boneless (we do not know why) but he certainly was not spineless. He went on to wreak havoc and destruction throughout England, Scotland and, eventually, Ireland where, known as Imharr, he appears to have gone on a tomb raiding spree in the sacred Boyne Valley breaking open the ancient mounds including New Grange – but that, as they say, is another story!

## Brother Jocundus

This story has all the signs of being an early Victorian version of a much-travelled story, relocated to York. It certainly is rather ignorant of both monasteries and Medieval York, where St Leonard's was a hospice for the sick, not a monastery as such. The historically minded might be interested in the following short description of it.

It was founded, according to tradition, by King Athelstan on his return from the battle of Brunanburgh. He built a small hospital for the poor, to the west of the minster, and generously endowed it with one thrave (twenty sheaves) from every plough being used in the diocese. (The thraves were known as Petercorn.) It was run by a master and chaplains; some ordained monks from the minster, some secular. There were also about eight sisters; some ordained and some secular. They cared for about 180 sick or incapacitated people, who were cared for until they either died or were sufficiently recovered to work. Mothers will be pleased to know that two sisters were assigned to a special room for abandoned babies who were fed with the milk of two cows.

It is hard for us to realise how strong anti-Catholic feeling was in England in the past – the nearest equivalent would be some people's attitude to Muslims. The idea of the walled-up monk or nun, popular in Gothic novels, was a common Protestant theme arising perhaps from anti-Catholic propaganda, perhaps just from ignorance. There are several ghost stories that rely on this idea. In fact, the death penalty was a secular not a religious punishment (although walling-up was never on any statute book). As it happens there are actually punishments specified for St Leonards, of which the most severe appears to be temporary imprisonment in a room at the hospital and penance until 'signs of amendment' were seen. Brother Jocundus would have got off lightly.

## The Book of Fate

This is another story that has been located in York and Scarborough to give it authenticity. It is much closer to a traditional wonder tale than most of the stories in this book. The Book of Fate is an unusual addition. As in the Greek myth of Oedipus, it demonstrates how the attempt to avoid a particular destiny actually results in it being brought about. The finding of the ring in the fish appears in countless tales.

A version of this story can be found in Richard Blakeborough's *Wit, Character, Folklore and Customs of the North Riding of Yorkshire* under the chapter Children's Lore. He points out that it is related to various other European stories including one of the Brothers Grimm. Unfortunately, he does not say where he got it from.

I got my version from H. Gee's *Folk Tales of Yorkshire*.

### Robin Hood and the Knight

This story is found in 'A Geste of Robyn Hode', one of the first printed accounts of the outlaw, probably produced at the beginning of the sixteenth century. However, his origins can be traced back as far as the thirteenth century.

The tales seem to have been transmitted by the oral storytellers and entertainers employed by noble houses throughout the country. Robin was included in plays and Christmas revels and was so well known that impersonating him on special occasions was popular – even on one occasion at St Mary's Abbey! (*See* J.C. Holt's *Robin Hood*, Thames and Hudson, 1989.)

### Dick Turpin

The truth of any criminal's life is difficult to verify, but Dick Turpin's certainly appears to have been rather squalid. His old romantic image probably came from a completely different man named John 'Swift Nick' Nevinson, who lived before Turpin was born. It is from 'Swift Nick' that the myth of Turpin's ride from London to York was stolen. One morning in 1676 Nevinson robbed a homeward-bound sailor on the road outside Gads Hill, Kent and, deciding that he needed to establish an alibi, he set off on a ride that took him more than 190 miles in about fifteen hours. William Harrison Ainsworth included the exploit and attributed it to Turpin in his 1834 novel *Rookwood* (London: Richard Bentley, 1834). It is his particular version of the heroic highwayman that has endured when the pockmarked horse stealer has been forgotten.

There are trial accounts of so many of Turpin's associates that it is possible to follow his evil and violent exploits in considerable detail should one wish to do so – I have simplified the story somewhat, especially the convoluted way in which he was finally brought to trial.

There are a few thieves' cant words in the story, such as yellowboys. No doubt the real Turpin would have used a lot more.

There are many books on this horrible man and you can even see a version of him singing his (factually correct) song on YouTube.

### The Pirate Archbishop

This highly coloured and clearly mythical version of the life of Lancelot Blackburne comes from *Old Yorkshire* by William Smith (Morely: issued yearly from 1881). Almost everything in it is untrue (starting with his university, he went to Oxford, not Cambridge) but it is a genuine folk version of a well-loved celebrity of his day. He almost certainly was not a pirate, and he certainly was never called Muggins, but he does seem to have been employed as a spy by Charles II.

Horace Walpole, who knew him, wrote a description to a friend which shows that, pirate or not, he was definitely a character!

### The Death Pact

From *Old Yorkshire* Series I by William Smith.

### Further Reading

*Ghosts and Legends of Yorkshire* by Andy Roberts (Norwich: Jarrold Publishing, 1992)

*Folk Stories from the Yorkshire Dales* by Peter N. Walker (London: Robert Hale Ltd, 1991)

*Folk Tales from the North York Moors* by Peter N. Walker (London: Robert Hale Ltd, 1990)

*Yorkshire Legends and Traditions* by Revd Thomas Parkinson (London: E. Stock, 1888)

*The Hand of Glory and Further Grandfather's Tales* by R. Blakeborough and John Fairfax-Blakeborough (London: H. Frowde, 1924)